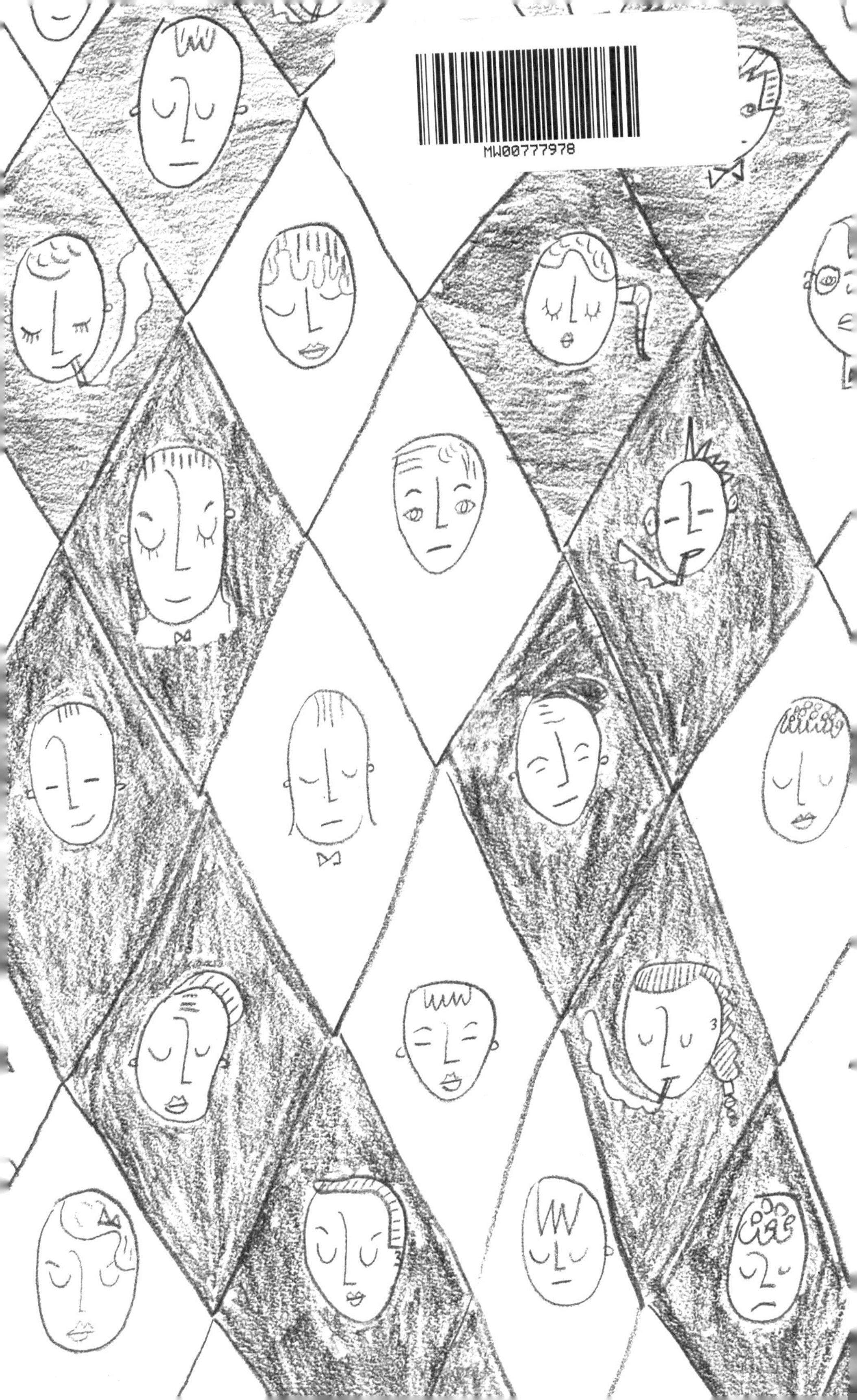

THANKS: Dan Nielsen, Erik Nelson, Alan Kizzah, Steve Lafler, Marynoel Strope (thanks x100), Simone Meltsen, Donny Adolph, Nate Jordan, T. Ed Bale, Sammy Harkham, Souther Salazar, Tesse Reklaw, Audrice Arp, Darwin Smith, Stephanie Wakefield, Delaine Derry Green, Ron Rege Jr., Sekhou Sundiata, Rebecca Chace, Jonathan Bennett, David Heatley, Sarah Janssen, Carley Moore, Lynda Schor, Matt Hannah, Jack Turnbull, Eric Blanc, Leo Makam, Chris Waldron, Anne E. Moore, Dirk Deppey, Tesse Hamm, Robert Davis, and Jennifer Moffitt

ALSO, thanks to the following true artistic inspirations: Maurice Sendak, Saul Steinberg CV, Lois Lenski, Ruth Chrisman Gannett, Alice Neel, Henri Matisse (DDD), Lynda Barry, John Porcellino, Frank O'Hara, Richard Brautigan, Emile Zola, Gabrielle Bell, Gustave Flaubert, Stevie L. Kohler, Ray Johnson, Joseph Cornell, Holly Woodlawn, Khaela M. Ca.Hua, The Blow), Thelonious Monk (DD), Hans Arp (DDDDD), Charlotte Salomon H.A. Rey, Dr. Seuss, George Selden, Garth Williams, William Steig, thousands more

SPECIAL PRODUCTION ASSISTANCE THANKS: Paul Pereira, Chris Eckert, Andrice Arp, Tesse Reklaw, Dan Zettwoch and Dylan "Nicest Guy in Comics" Williams.

THIS BOOK IS FOR: My mom (who made it okay for me to make and love art), my dad (who fights for every noble cause, that's his art), and my brothers Christopher + Dominic. I love you all more then I can say.

All of "Christina and Charles" is © Austin English, 2005 A.D. [Portions of "The Tape" are based on the book "The Gospel According to Jesus" by Stephen Mitchell, HarperCollins 19? This book was published by sparkplug comicbooks in Portland, OR.
www.sparkplugcomicbooks.com

Printed with care at Westcan, in the heart of the St.Boniface
Industrial Park, Winnipeg, Canada

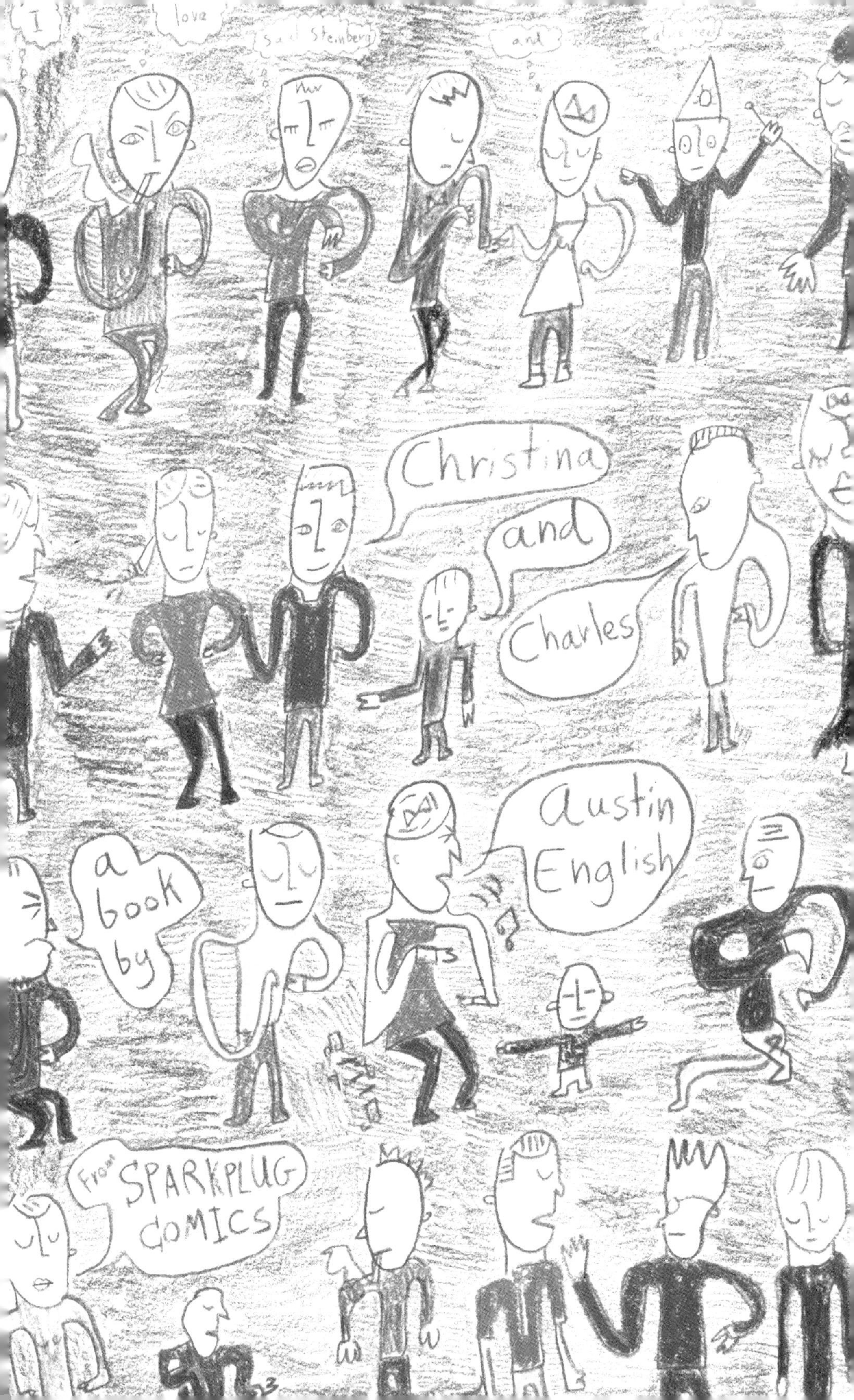

I
love
Saul Steinberg
and
Christina
and
Charles
a book by
Austin English
From SPARKPLUG COMICS

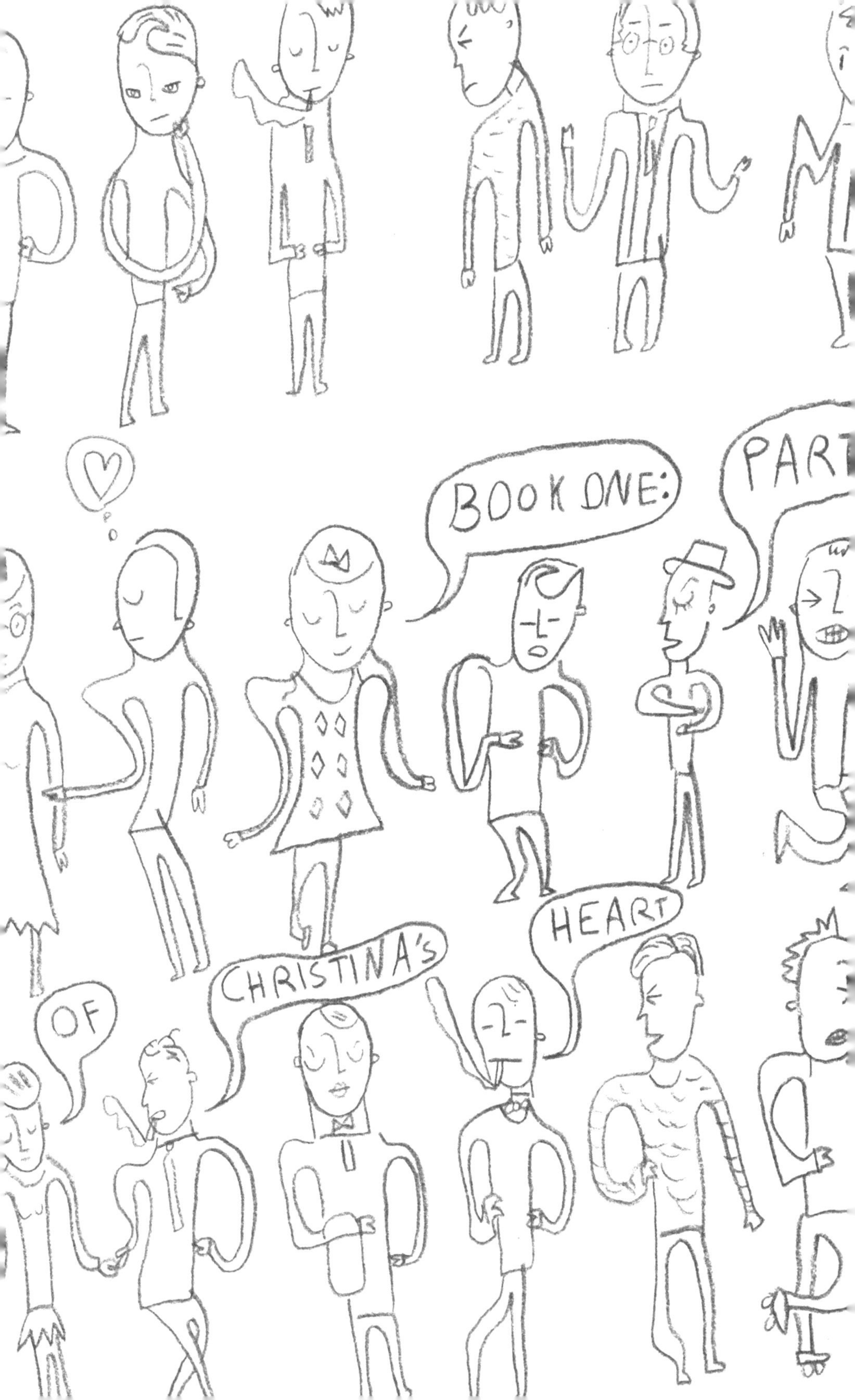
BOOK ONE:
PART
OF
CHRISTINA'S
HEART

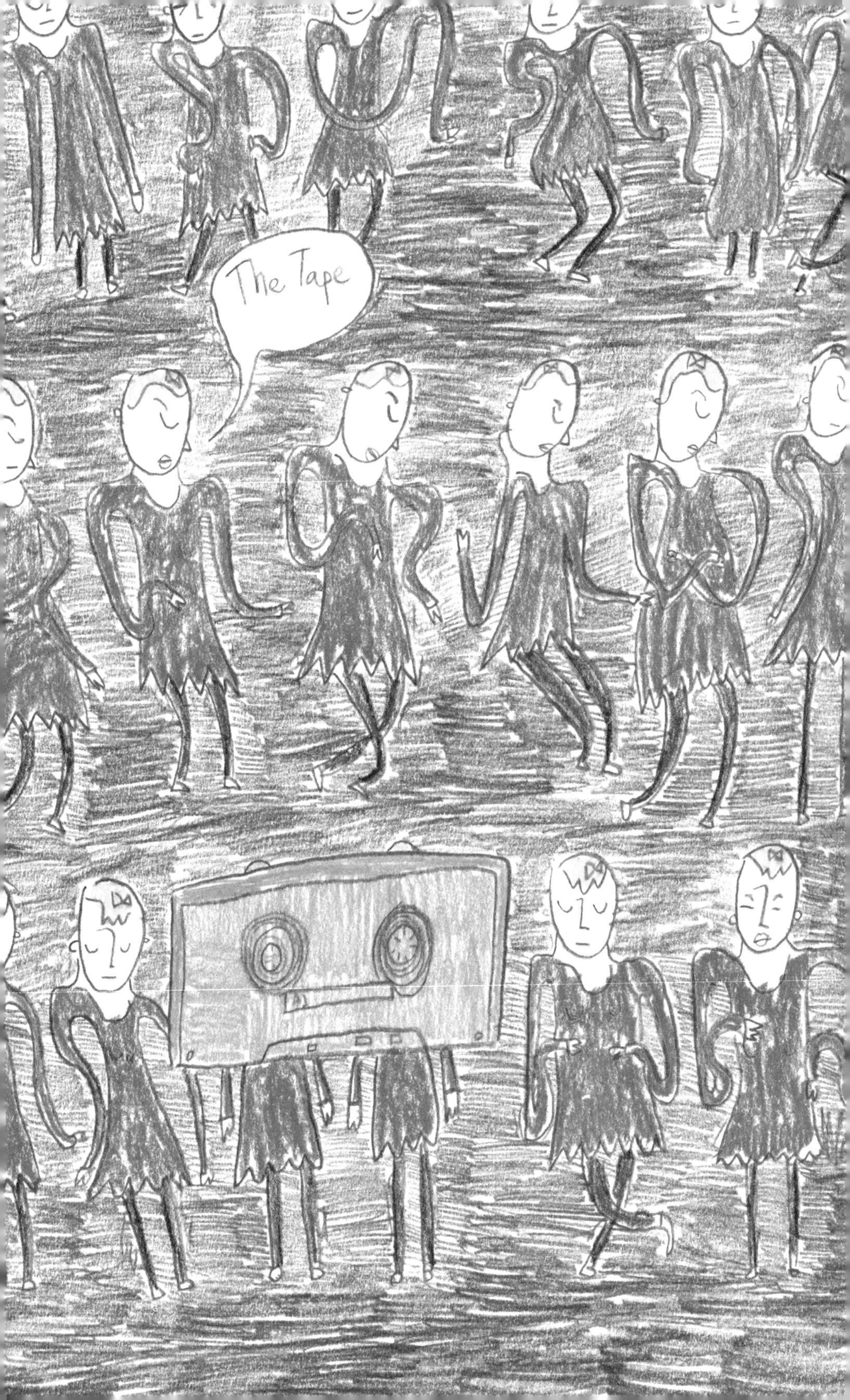
The Tape

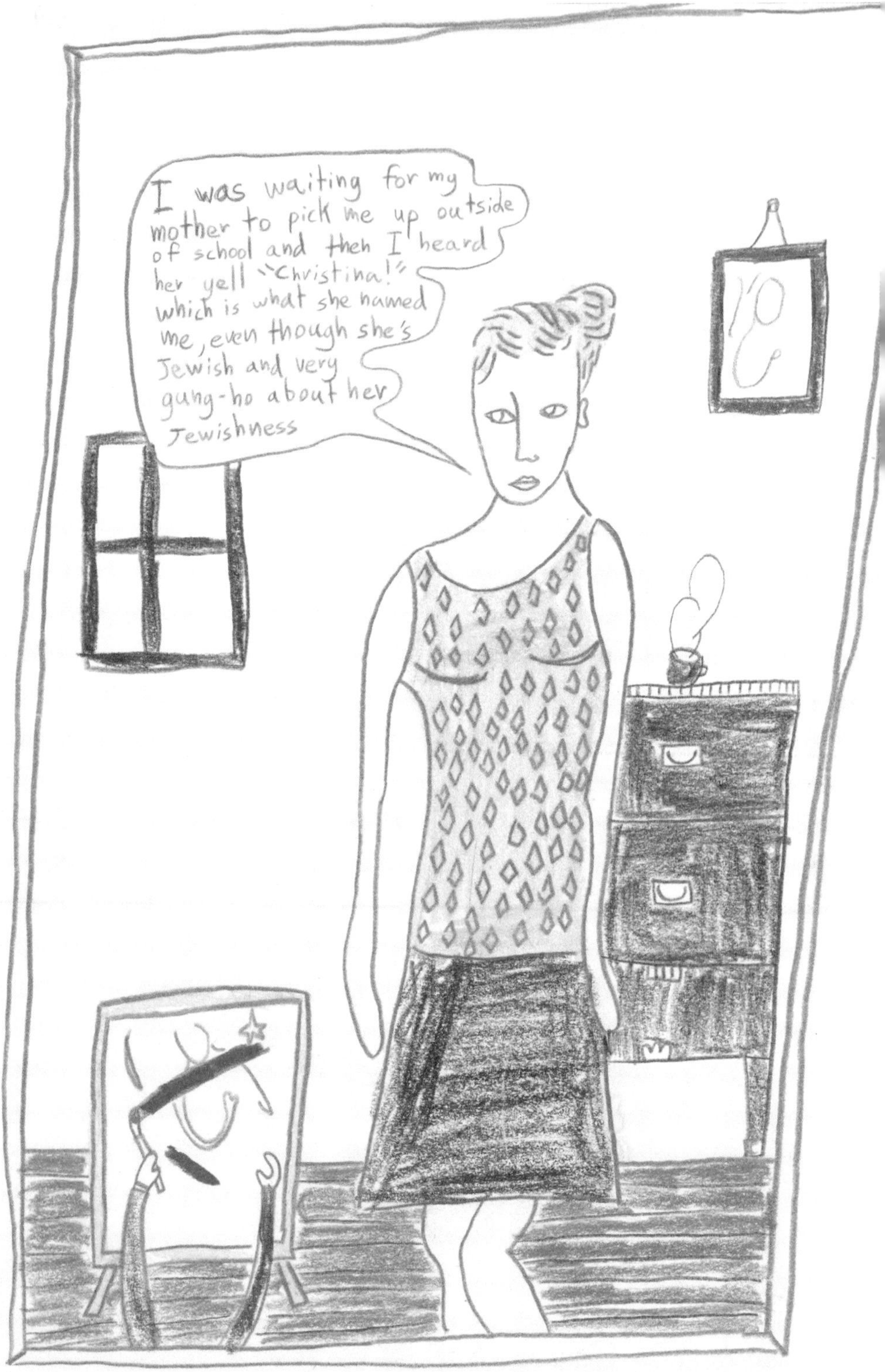
I was waiting for my mother to pick me up outside of school and then I heard her yell "Christina!" which is what she named me, even though she's Jewish and very gung-ho about her Jewishness

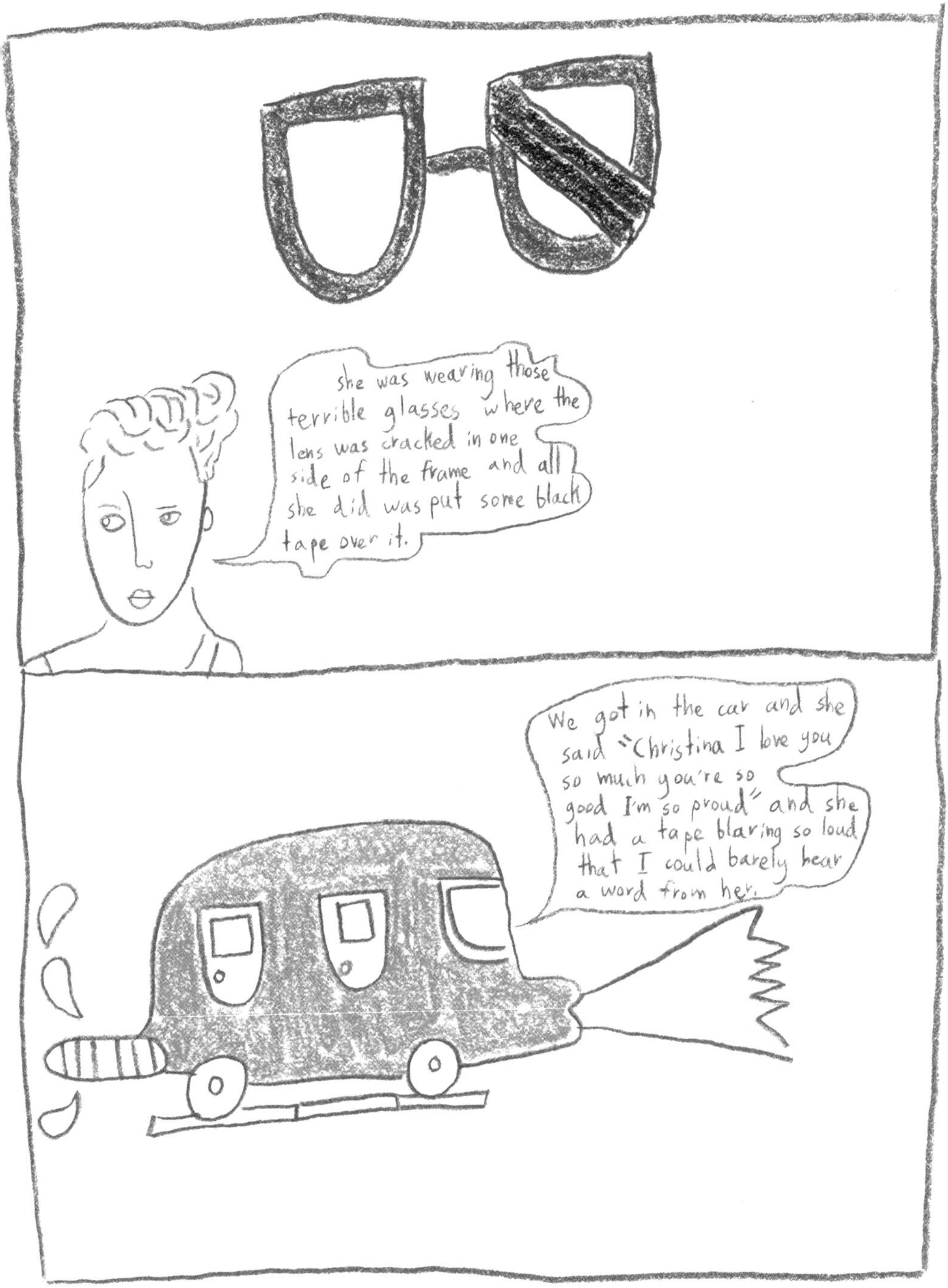
she was wearing those terrible glasses where the lens was cracked in one side of the frame and all she did was put some black tape over it.
We got in the car and she said "Christina I love you so much you're so good I'm so proud" and she had a tape blaring so loud that I could barely hear a word from her.

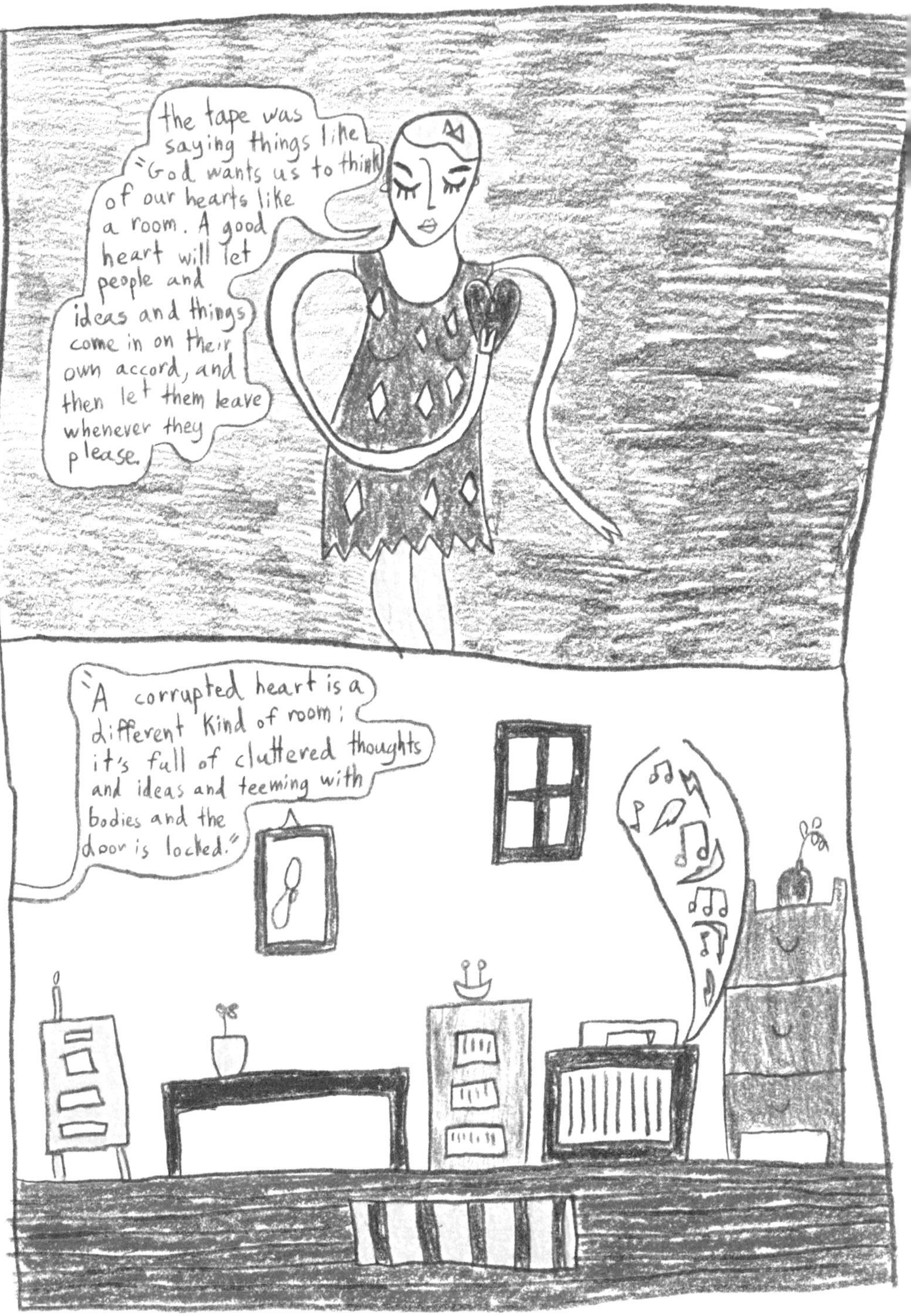
the tape was saying things like "God wants us to think of our hearts like a room. A good heart will let people and ideas and things come in on their own accord, and then let them leave whenever they please.
"A corrupted heart is a different kind of room; it's full of cluttered thoughts and ideas and teeming with bodies and the door is locked."

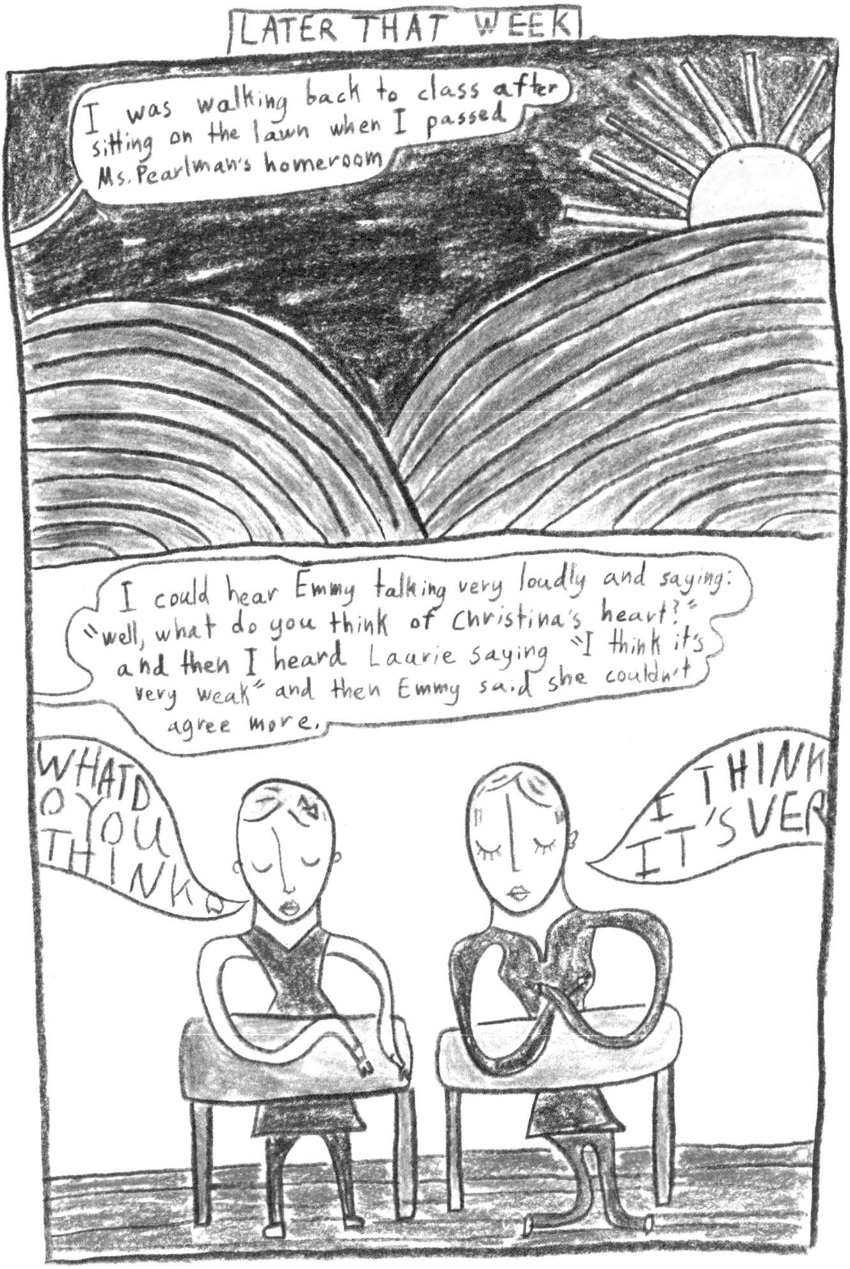
LATER THAT WEEK
I was walking back to class after sitting on the lawn when I passed Ms. Pearlman's homeroom
I could hear Emmy talking very loudly and saying: "well, what do you think of Christina's heart?" and then I heard Laurie saying "I think it's very weak" and then Emmy said she couldn't agree more.
WHAT DO YOU THINK
I THINK IT'S VER

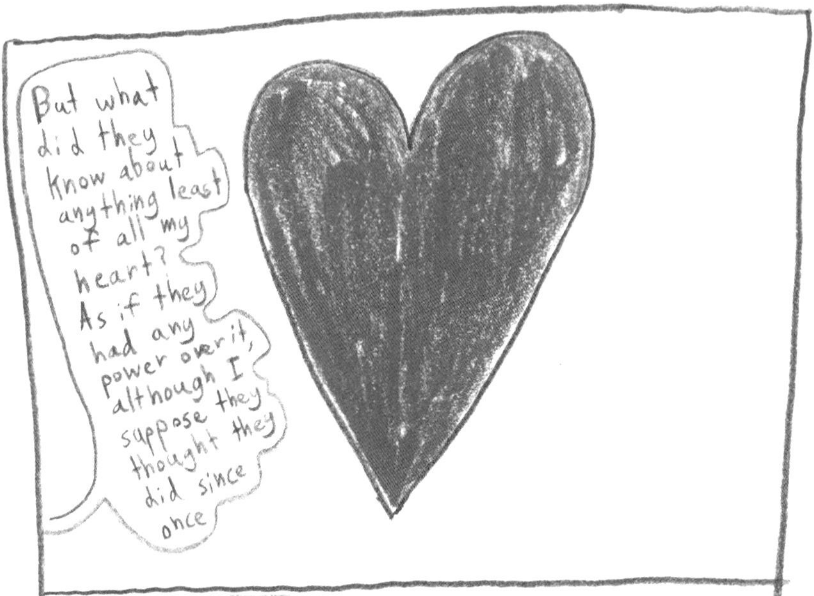
But what did they know about anything least of all my heart? As if they had any power over it, although I suppose they thought they did since once

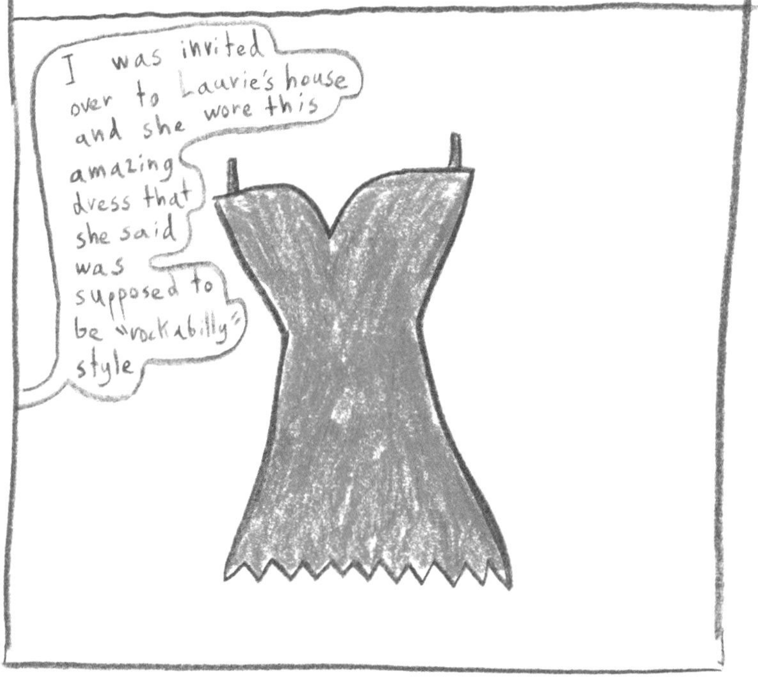
I was invited over to Laurie's house and she wore this amazing dress that she said was supposed to be "rockabilly" style

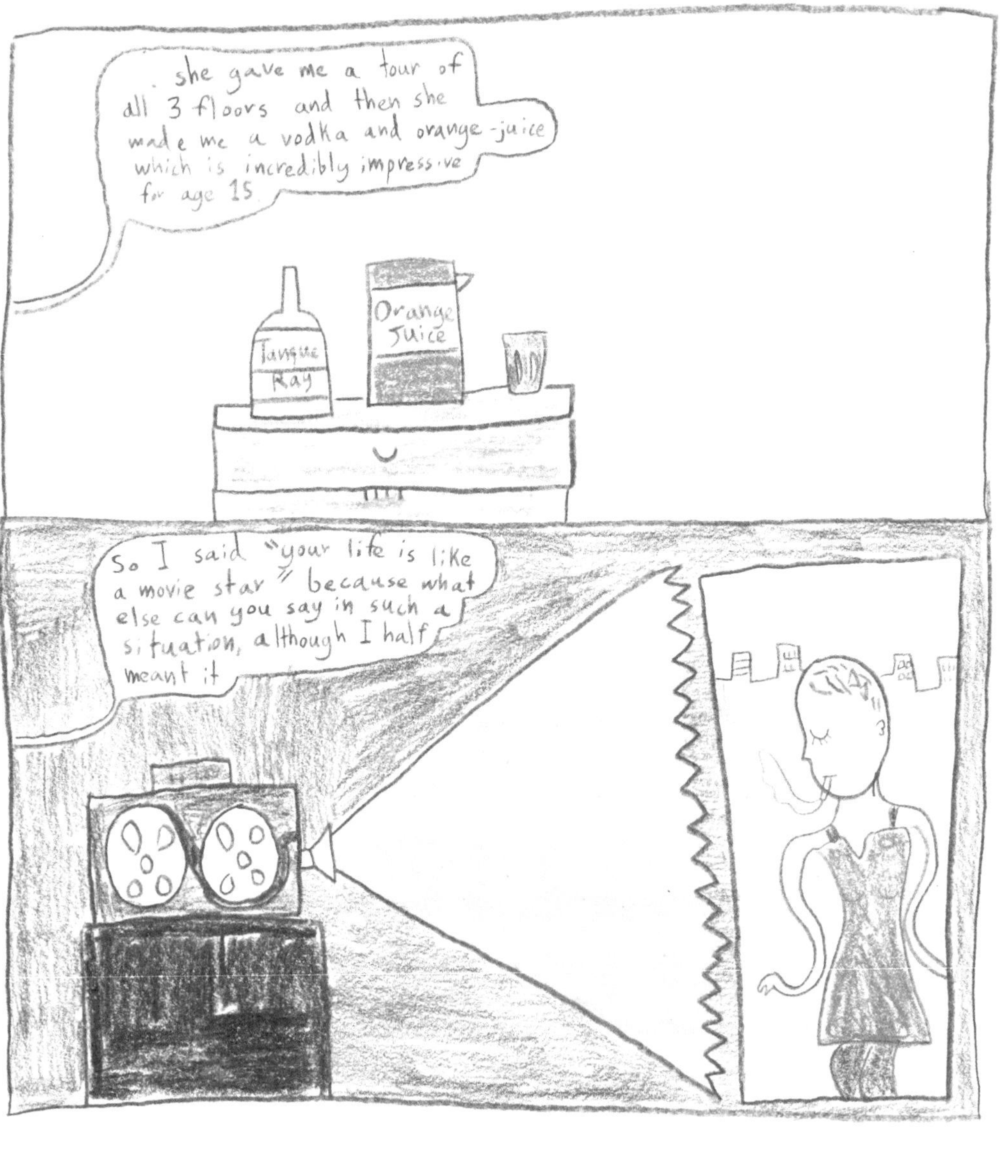
...she gave me a tour of all 3 floors and then she made me a vodka and orange-juice which is incredibly impressive for age 15
Tanque Ray
Orange Juice
So I said "your life is like a movie star" because what else can you say in such a situation, although I half meant it

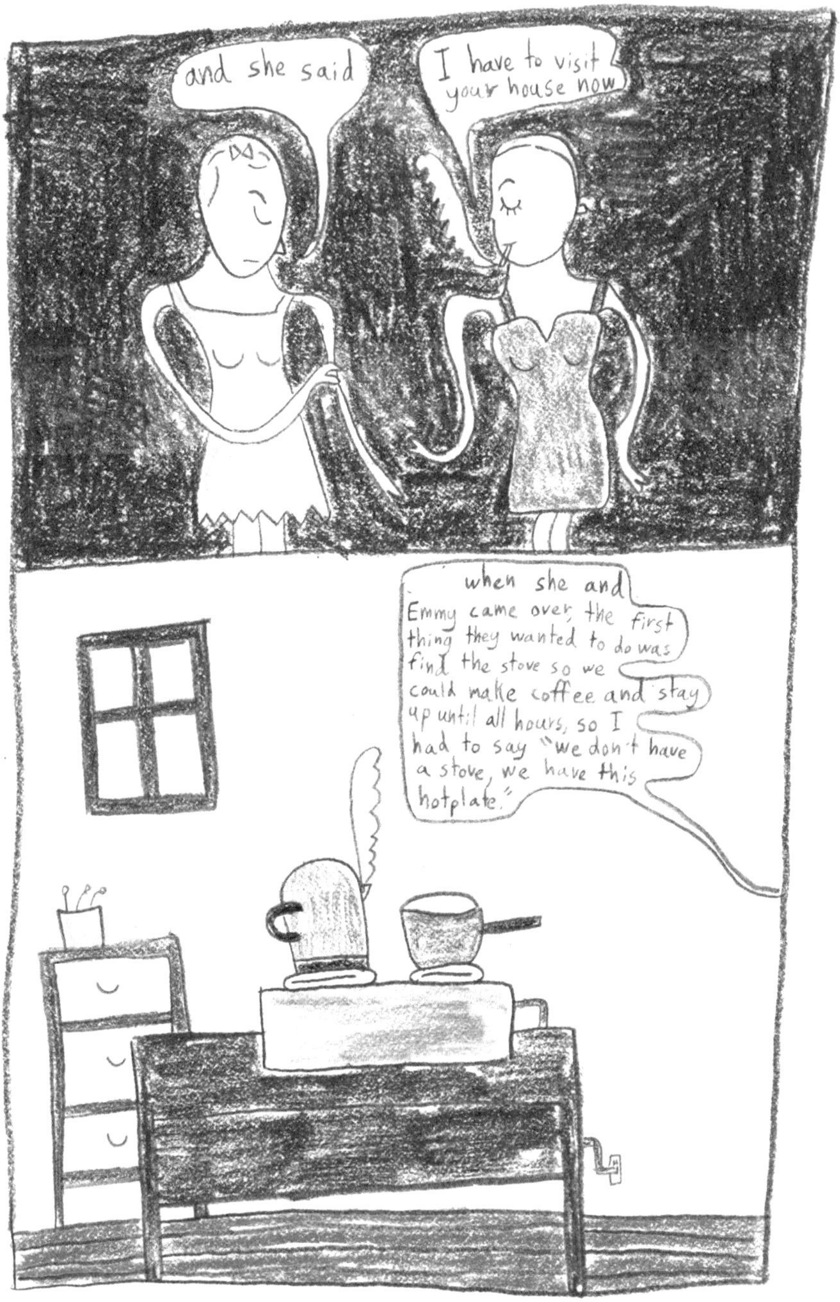
and she said
I have to visit your house now
when she and Emmy came over, the first thing they wanted to do was find the stove so we could make coffee and stay up until all hours, so I had to say "we don't have a stove, we have this hotplate."

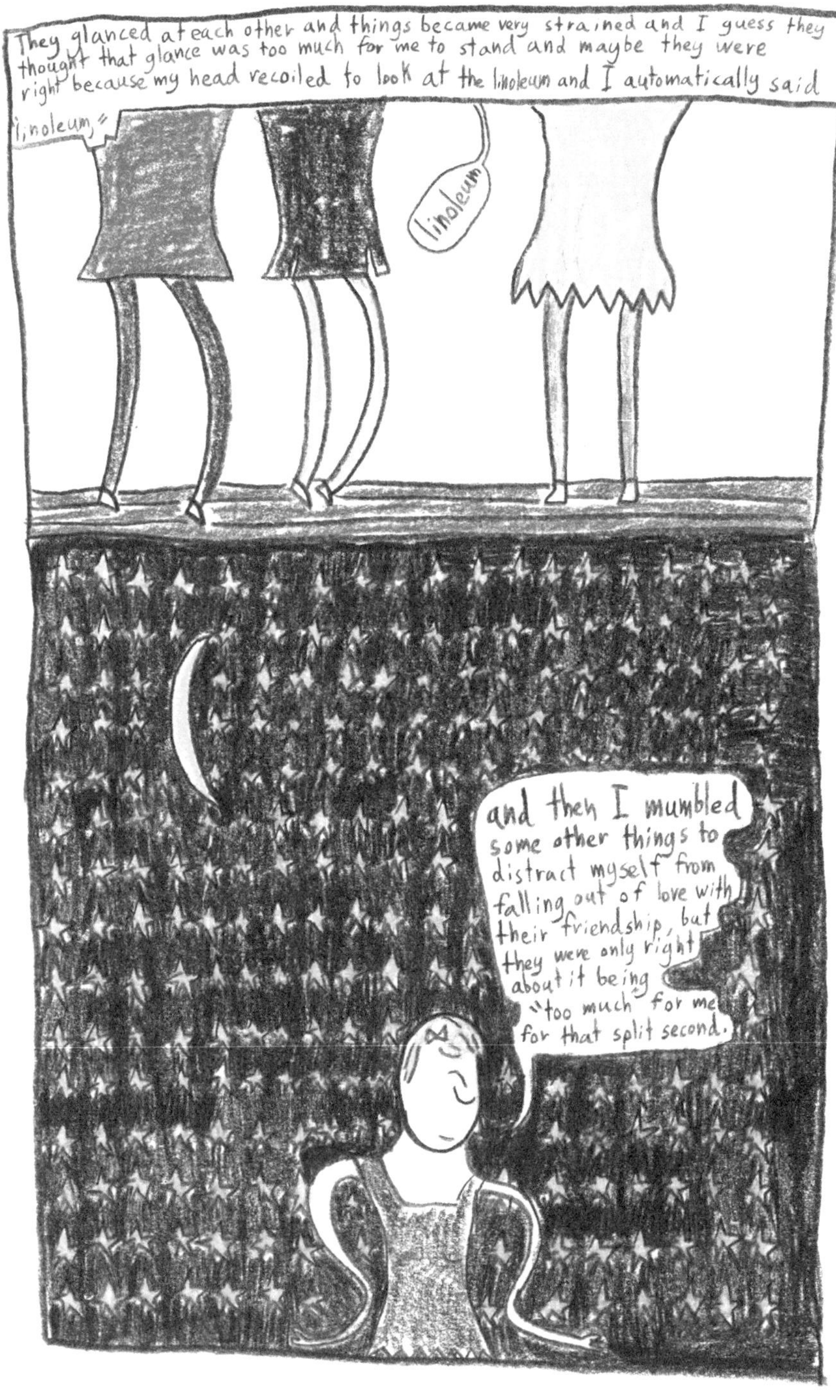
They glanced at each other and things became very strained and I guess they thought that glance was too much for me to stand and maybe they were right because my head recoiled to look at the linoleum and I automatically said
"linoleum,"
linoleum
and then I mumbled some other things to distract myself from falling out of love with their friendship, but they were only right about it being "too much" for me for that split second.

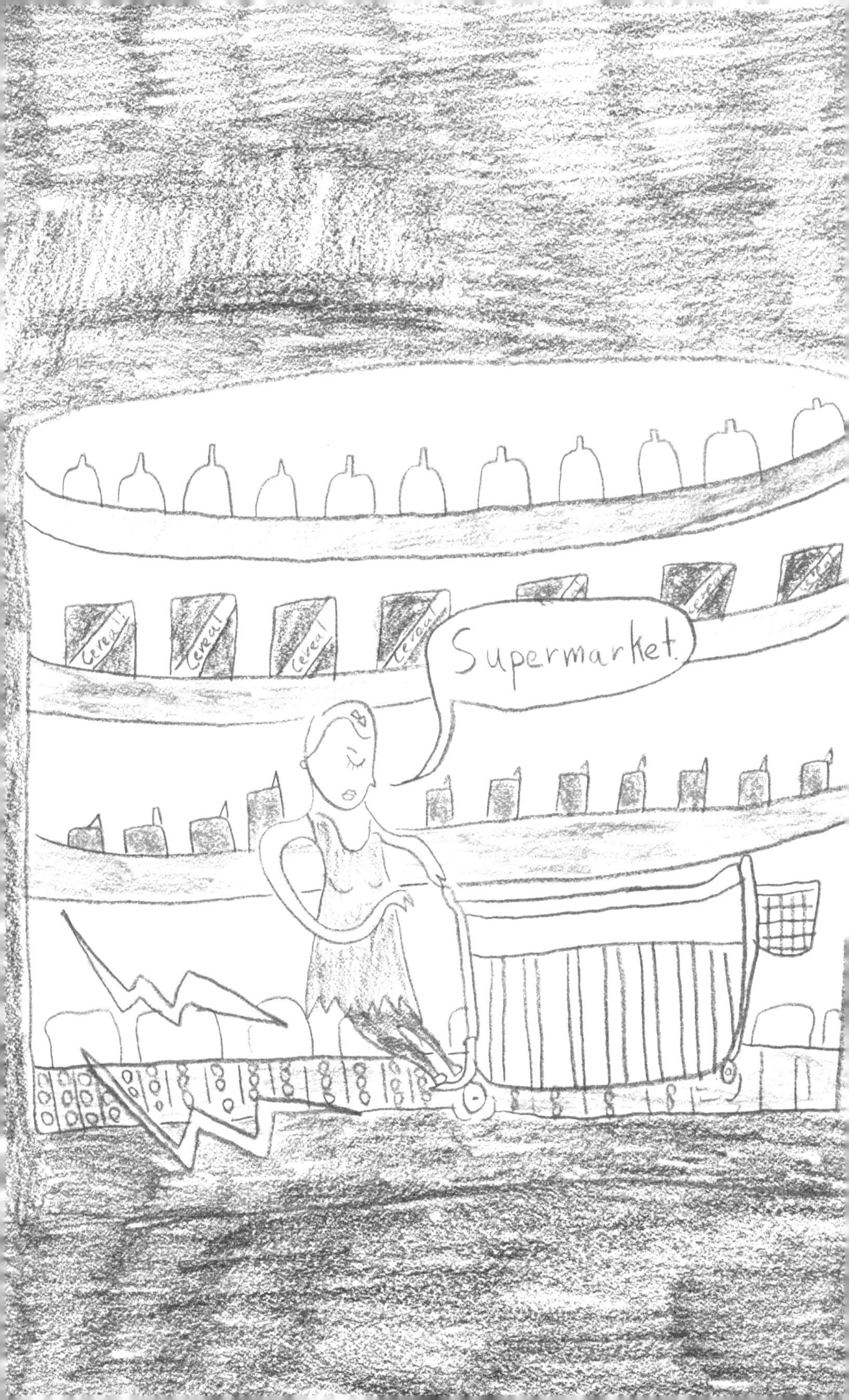
Supermarket.

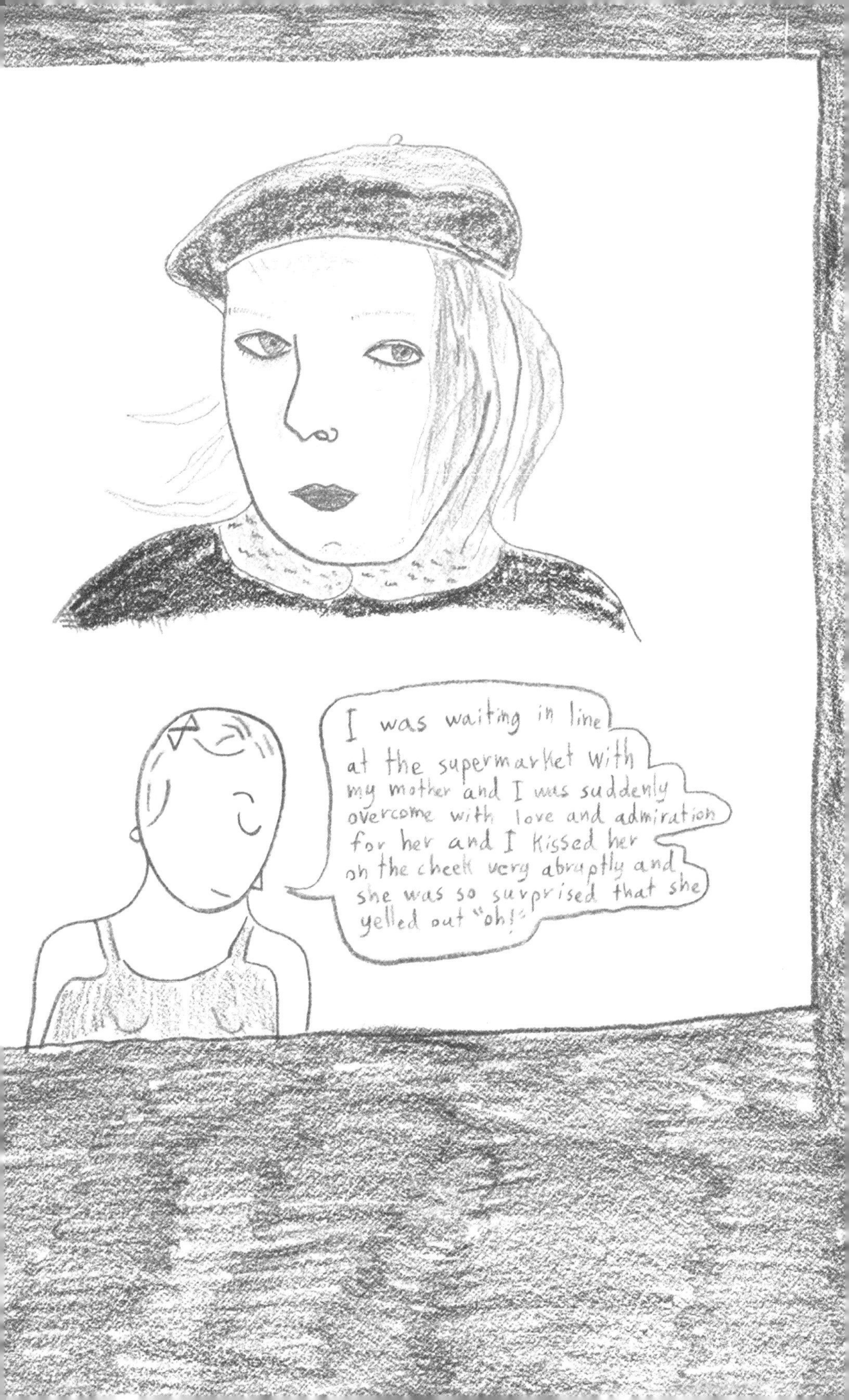
I was waiting in line at the supermarket with my mother and I was suddenly overcome with love and admiration for her and I kissed her on the cheek very abruptly and she was so surprised that she yelled out "oh!"

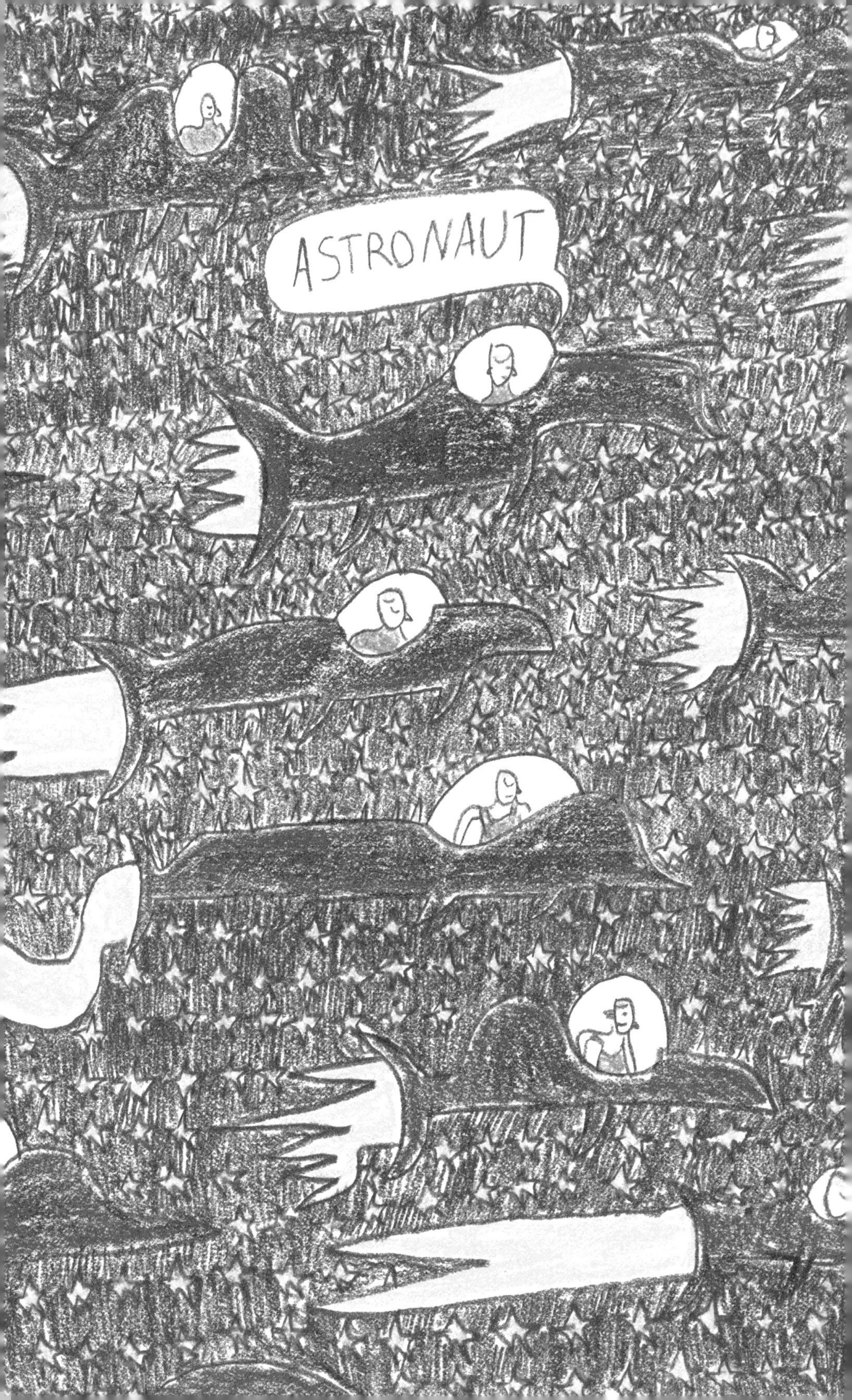
ASTRONAUT

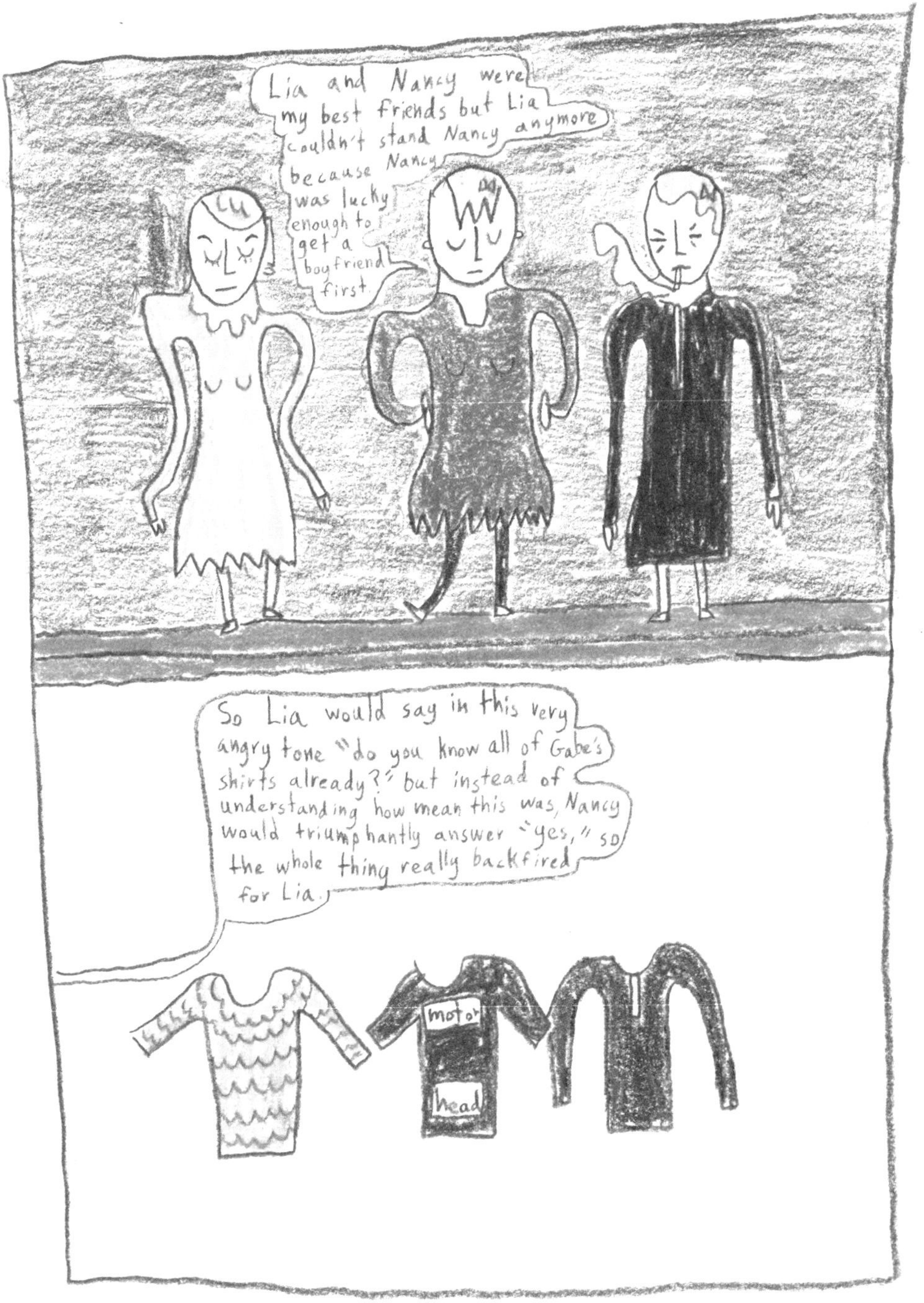
Lia and Nancy were my best friends but Lia couldn't stand Nancy anymore because Nancy was lucky enough to get a boyfriend first.
So Lia would say in this very angry tone "do you know all of Gabe's shirts already?" but instead of understanding how mean this was, Nancy would triumphantly answer "yes," so the whole thing really backfired for Lia.
motor
head

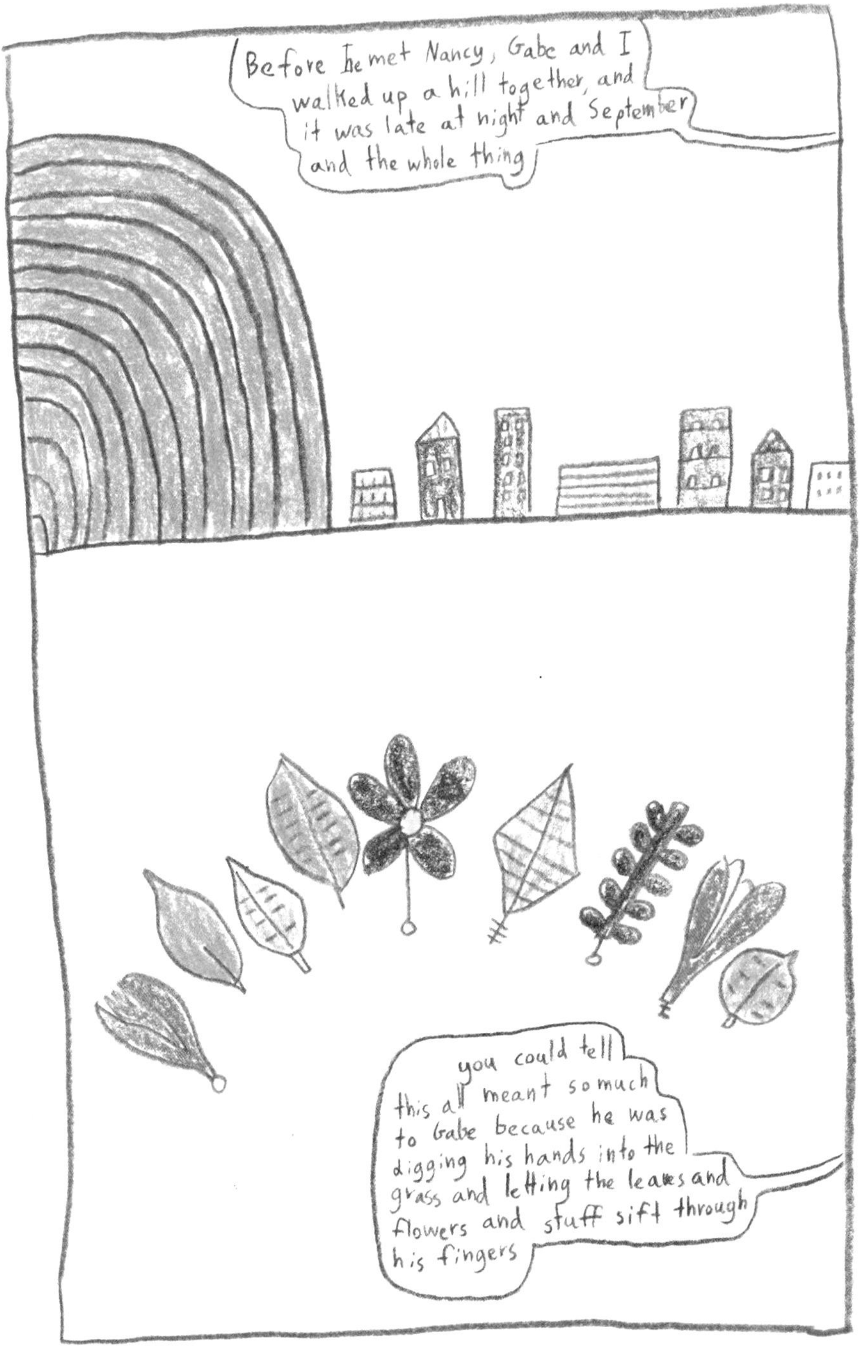
Before he met Nancy, Gabe and I walked up a hill together, and it was late at night and September and the whole thing
you could tell this all meant so much to Gabe because he was digging his hands into the grass and letting the leaves and flowers and stuff sift through his fingers

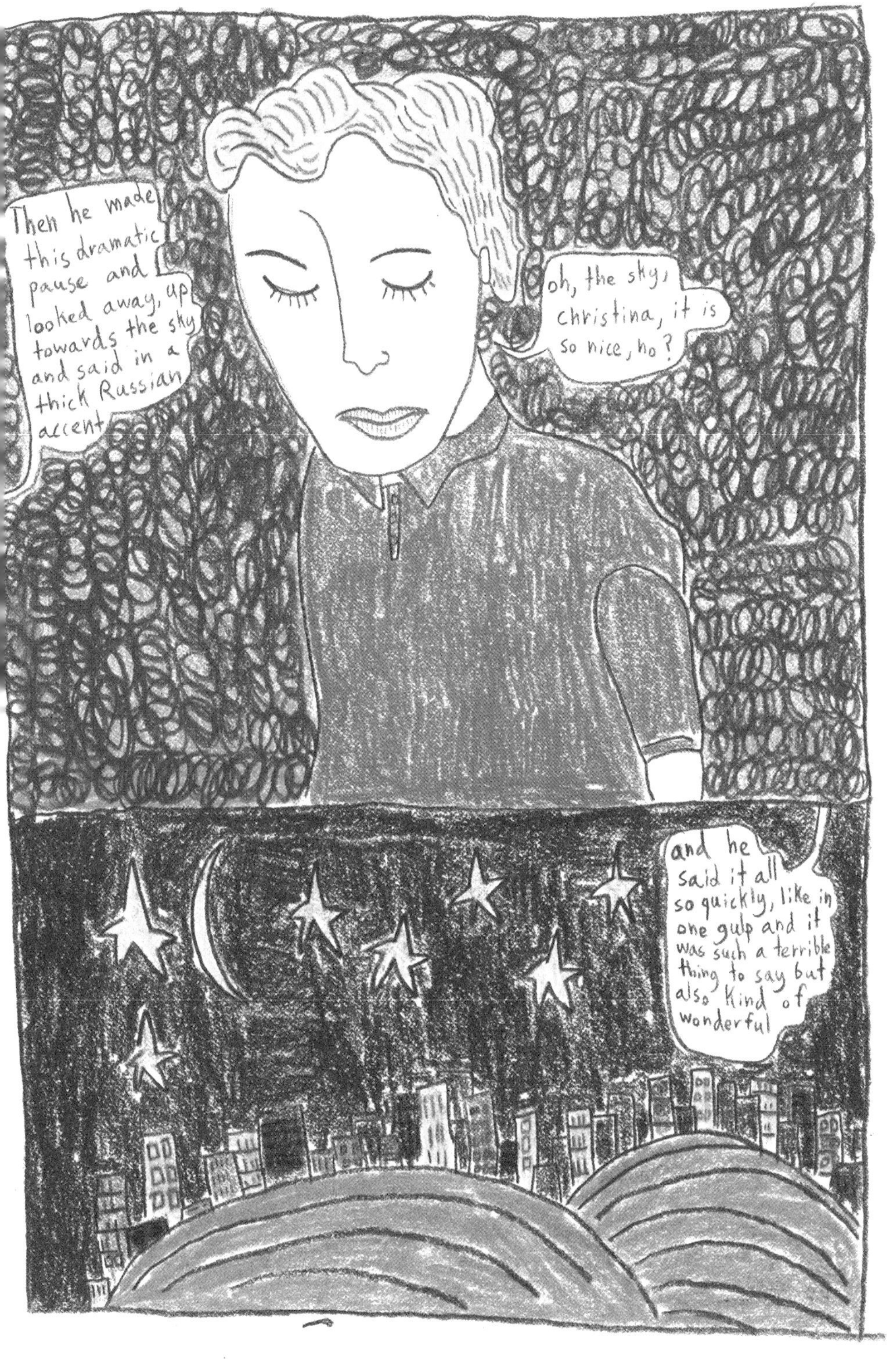
Then he made this dramatic pause and looked away, up towards the sky and said in a thick Russian accent
oh, the sky, christina, it is so nice, no?
and he said it all so quickly, like in one gulp and it was such a terrible thing to say but also kind of wonderful

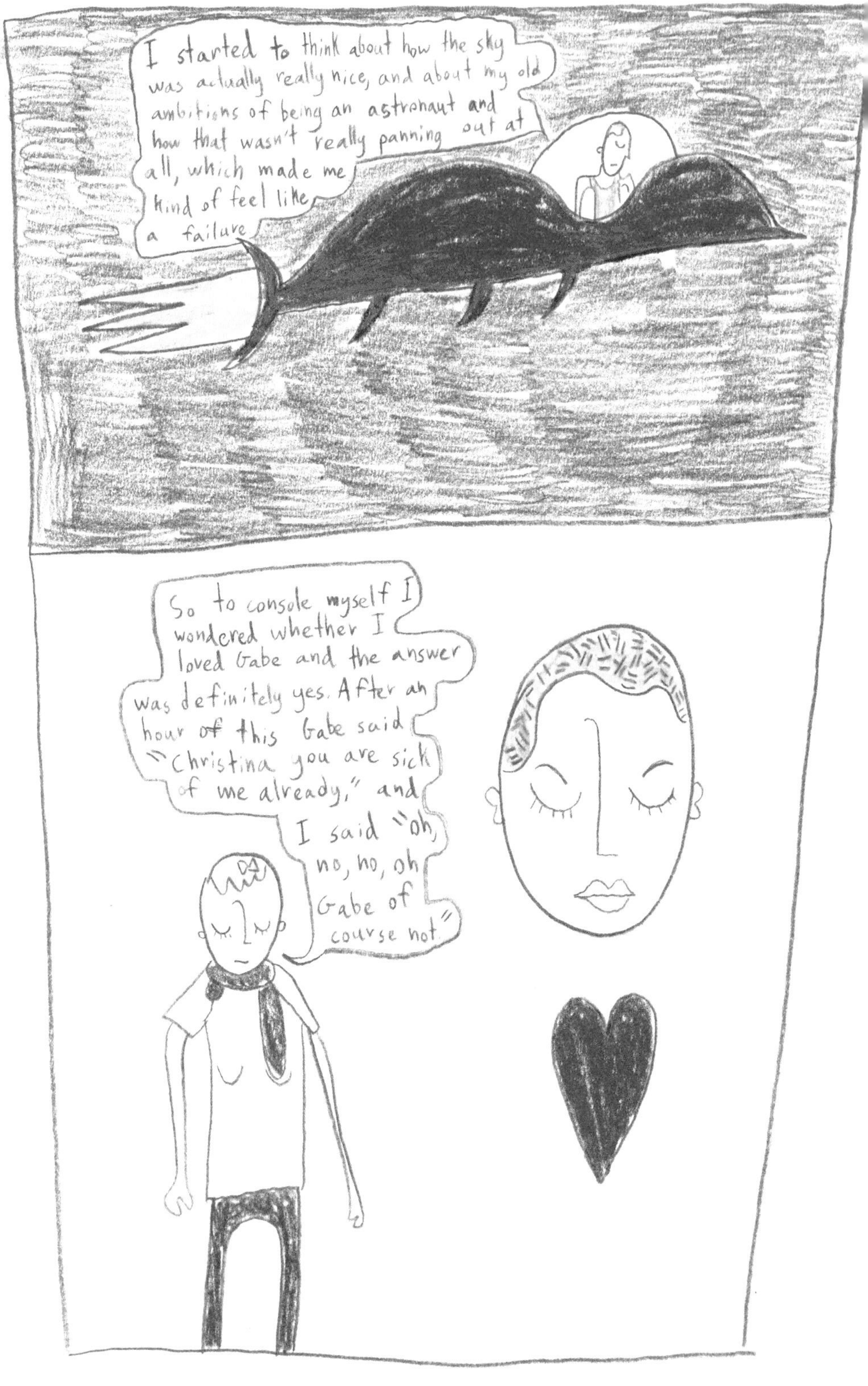
I started to think about how the sky was actually really nice, and about my old ambitions of being an astronaut and how that wasn't really panning out at all, which made me kind of feel like a failure
So to console myself I wondered whether I loved Gabe and the answer was definitely yes. After an hour of this Gabe said "Christina you are sick of me already," and I said "oh, no, no, oh Gabe of course not."

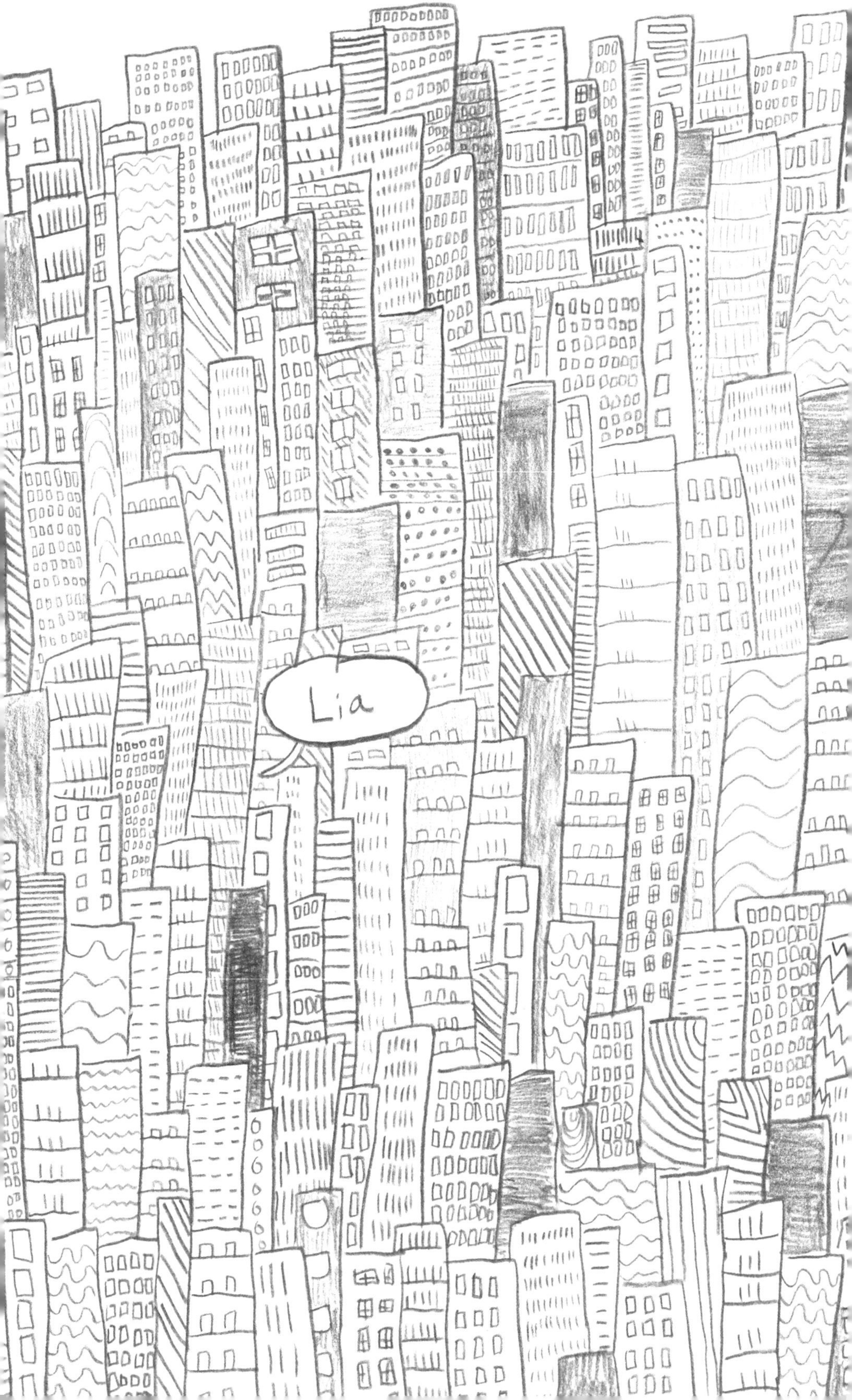
Lia

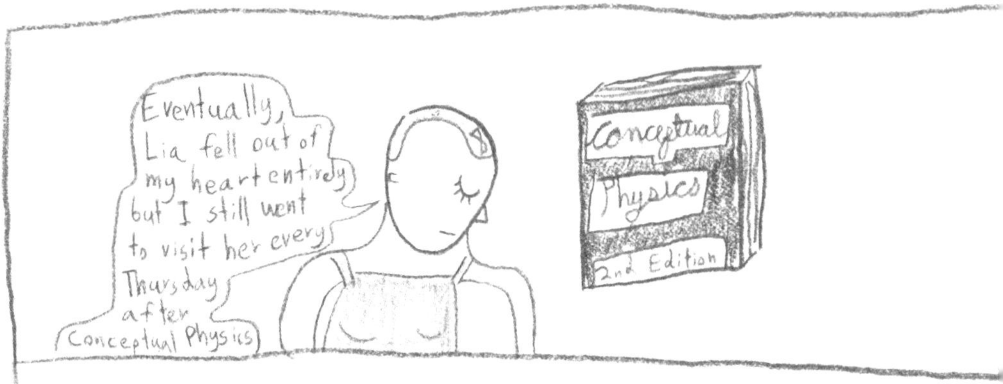
Eventually, Lia fell out of my heart entirely but I still went to visit her every Thursday after Conceptual Physics
Conceptual Physics
2nd Edition

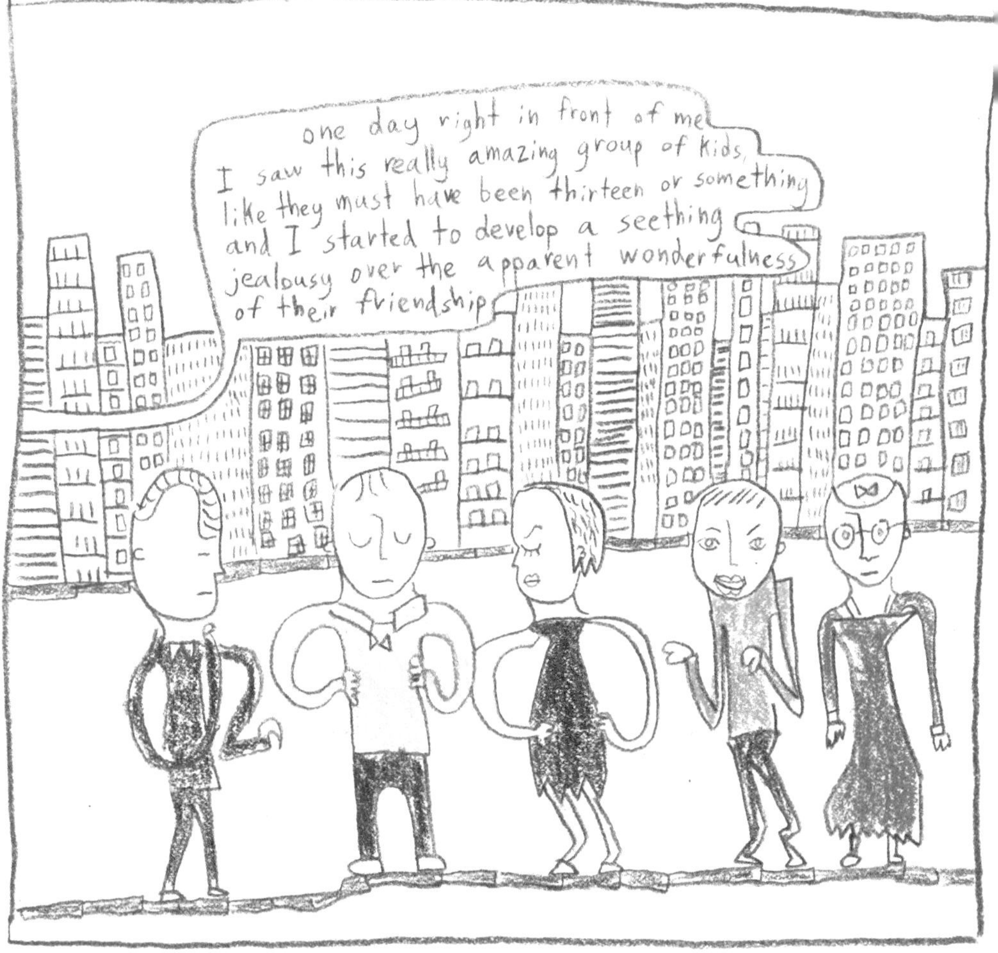
one day right in front of me I saw this really amazing group of kids, like they must have been thirteen or something and I started to develop a seething jealousy over the apparent wonderfulness of their friendship

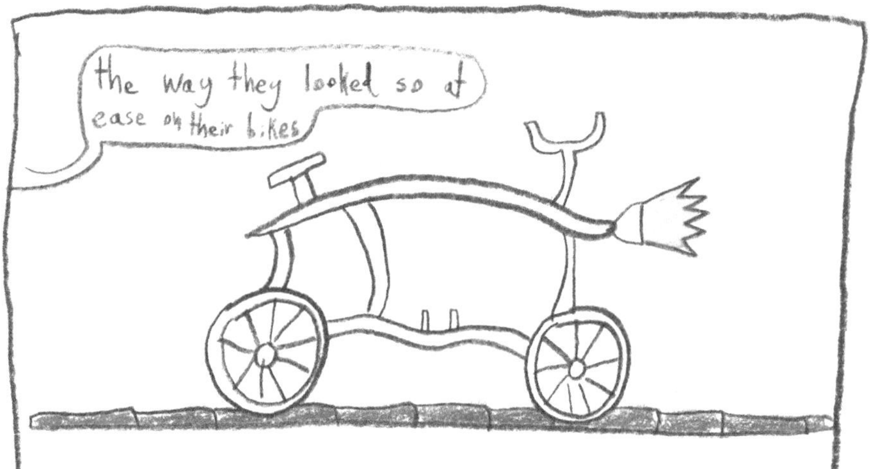
the way they looked so at ease on their bikes

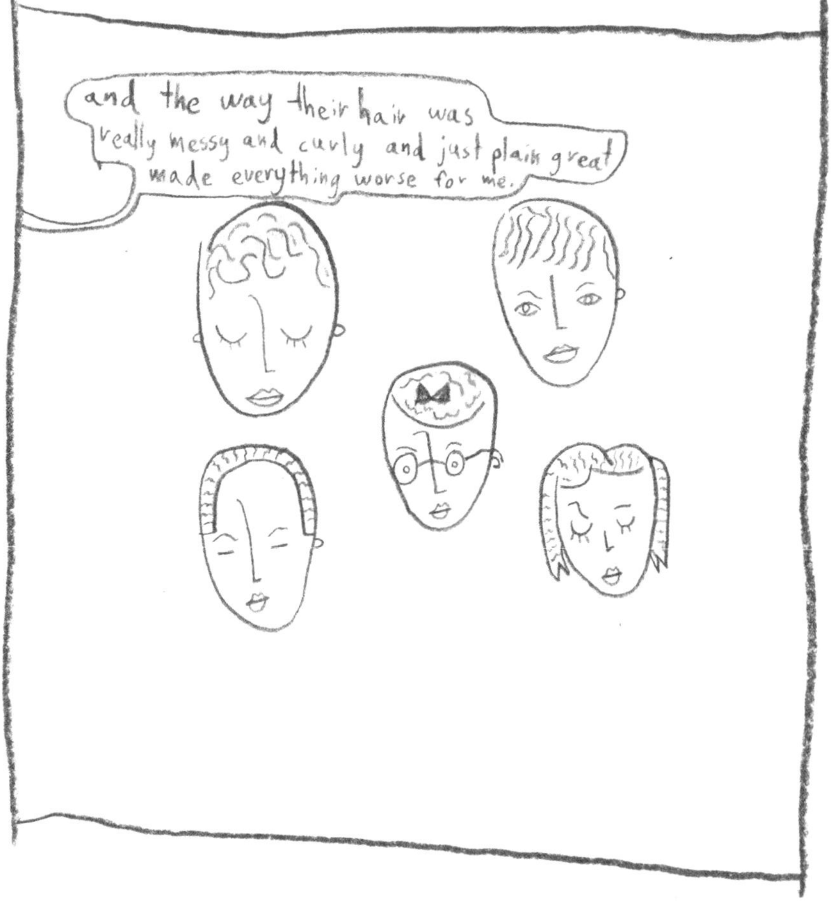
and the way their hair was really messy and curly and just plain great made everything worse for me.

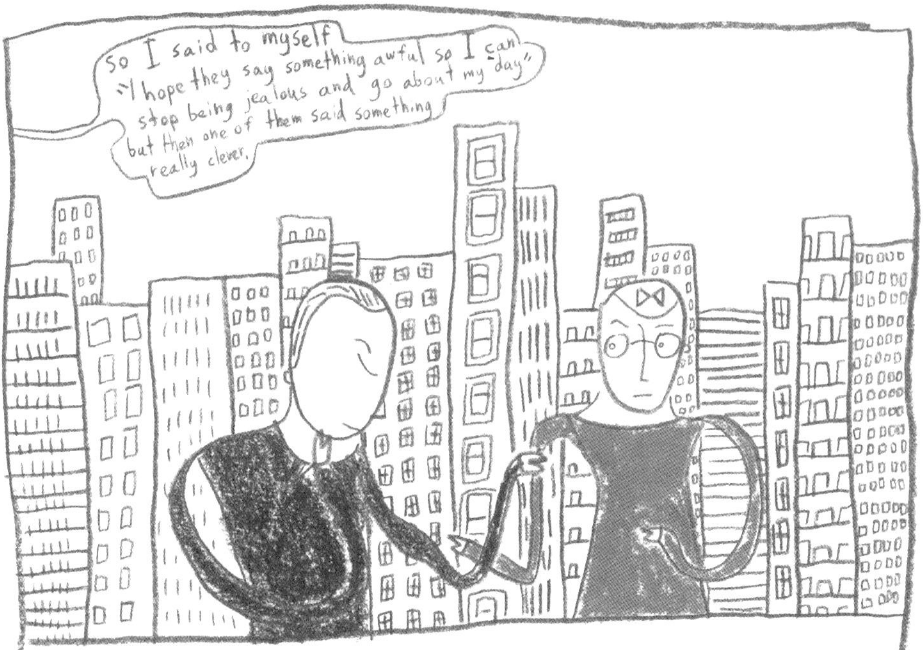
So I said to myself "I hope they say something awful so I can stop being jealous and go about my day" but then one of them said something really clever.

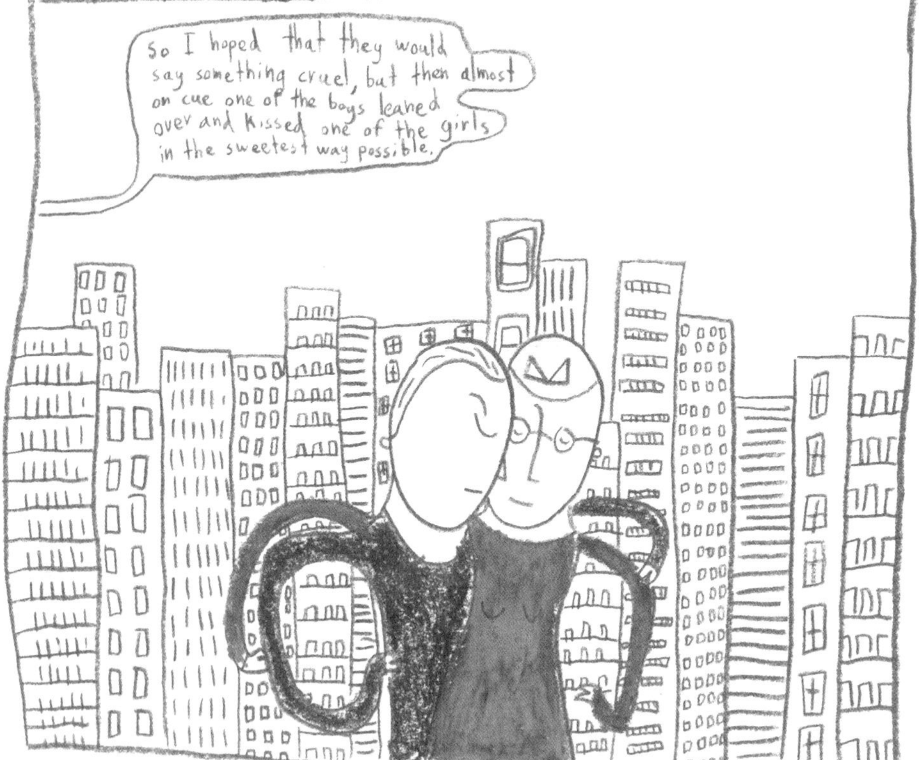
So I hoped that they would say something cruel, but then almost on cue one of the boys leaned over and kissed one of the girls in the sweetest way possible.

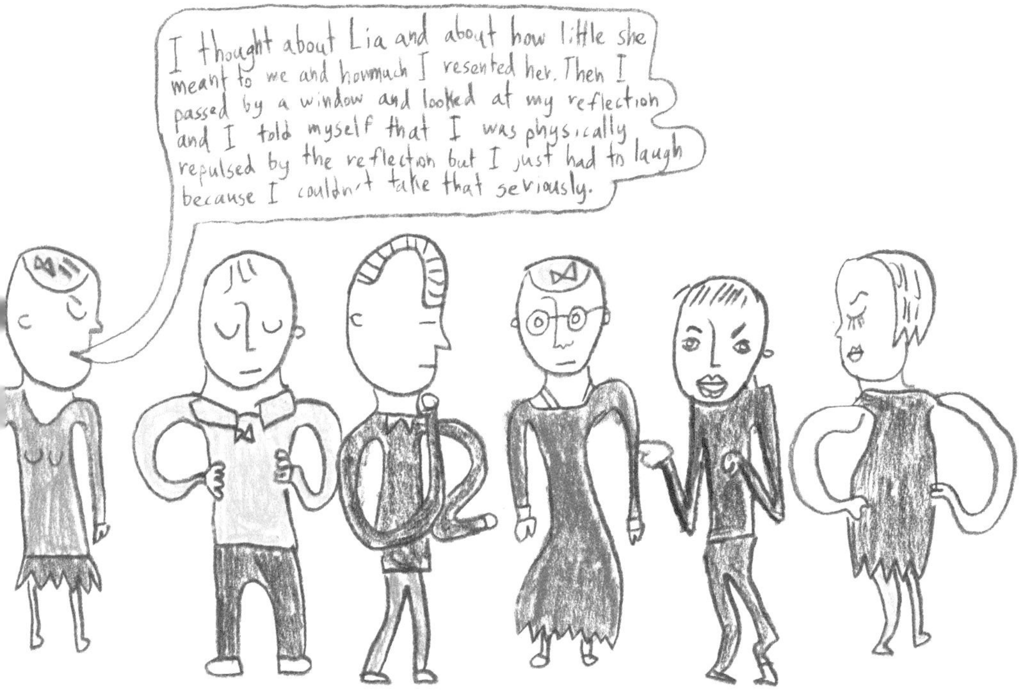
I thought about Lia and about how little she meant to me and howmuch I resented her. Then I passed by a window and looked at my reflection and I told myself that I was physically repulsed by the reflection but I just had to laugh because I couldn't take that seriously.

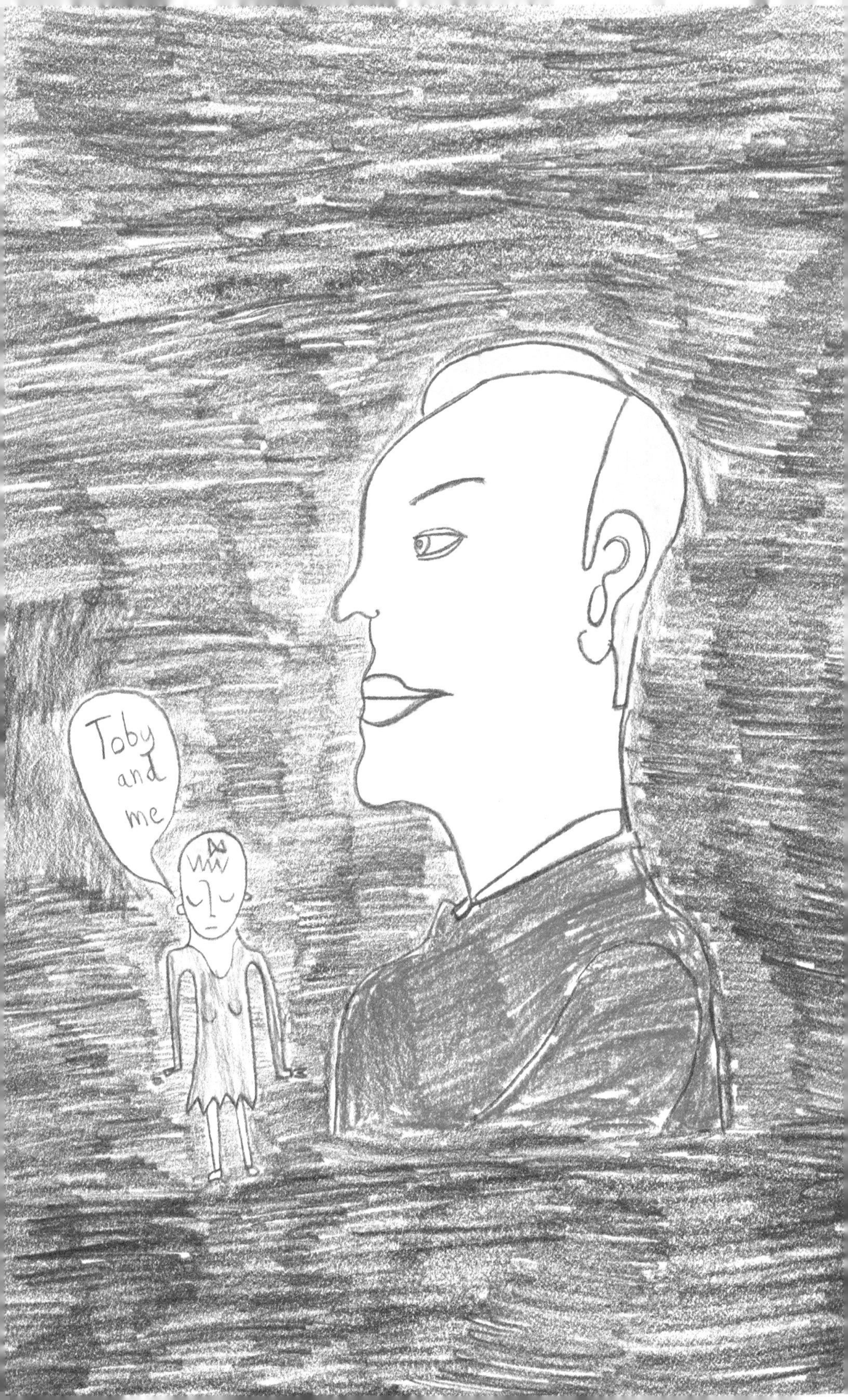
Toby and me

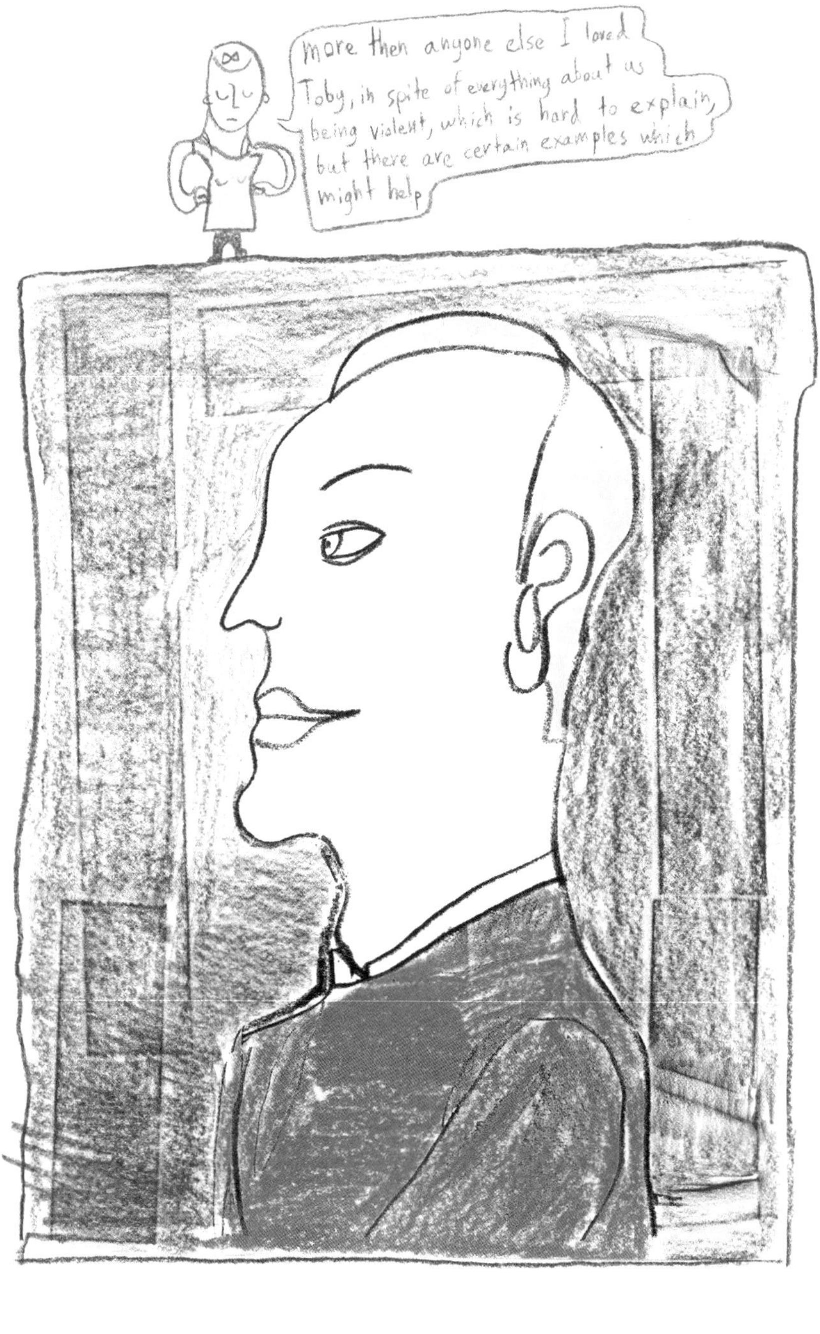
more then anyone else I loved Toby, in spite of everything about us being violent, which is hard to explain, but there are certain examples which might help

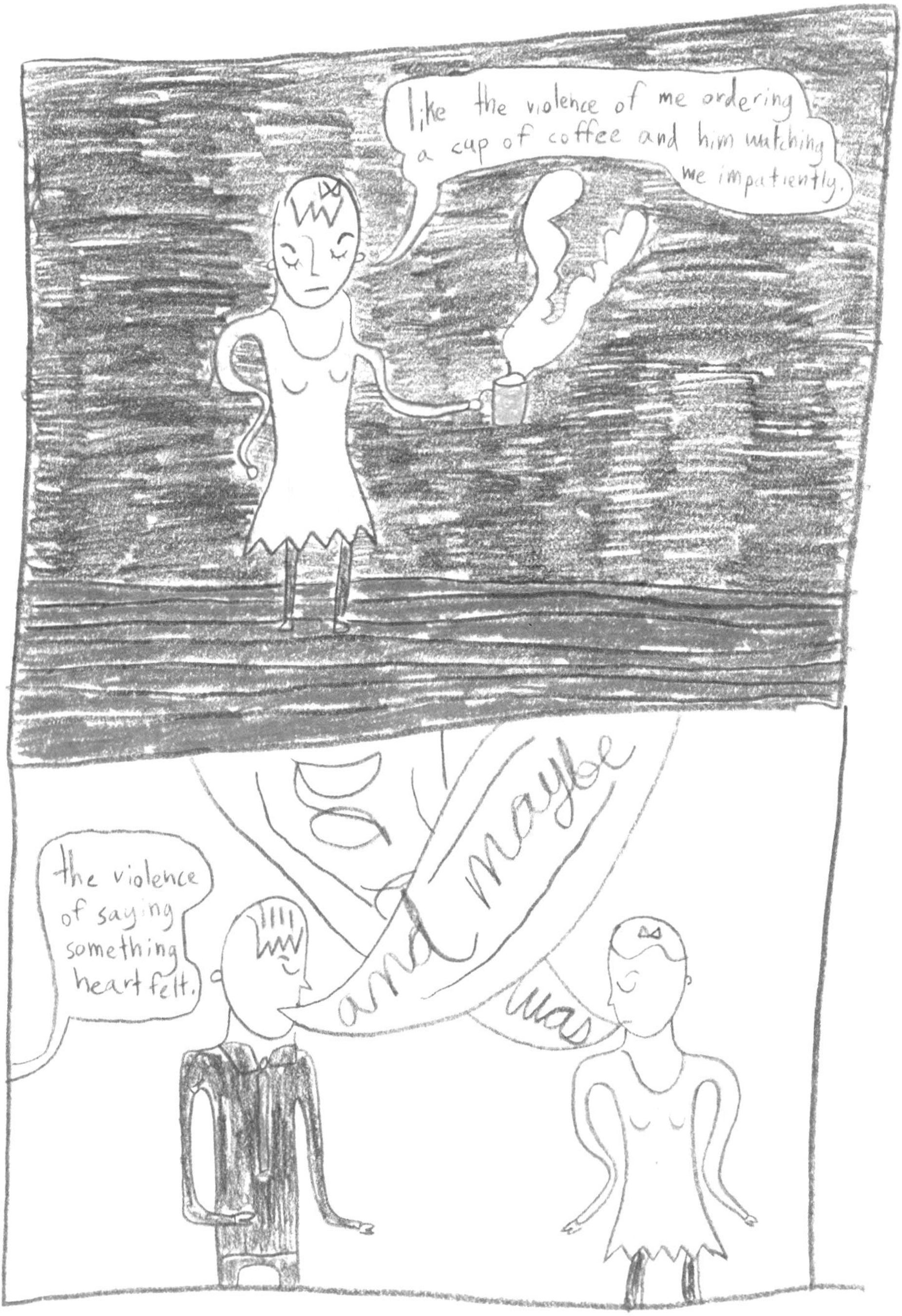
like the violence of me ordering a cup of coffee and him watching me impatiently.
the violence of saying something heartfelt.
and maybe
was

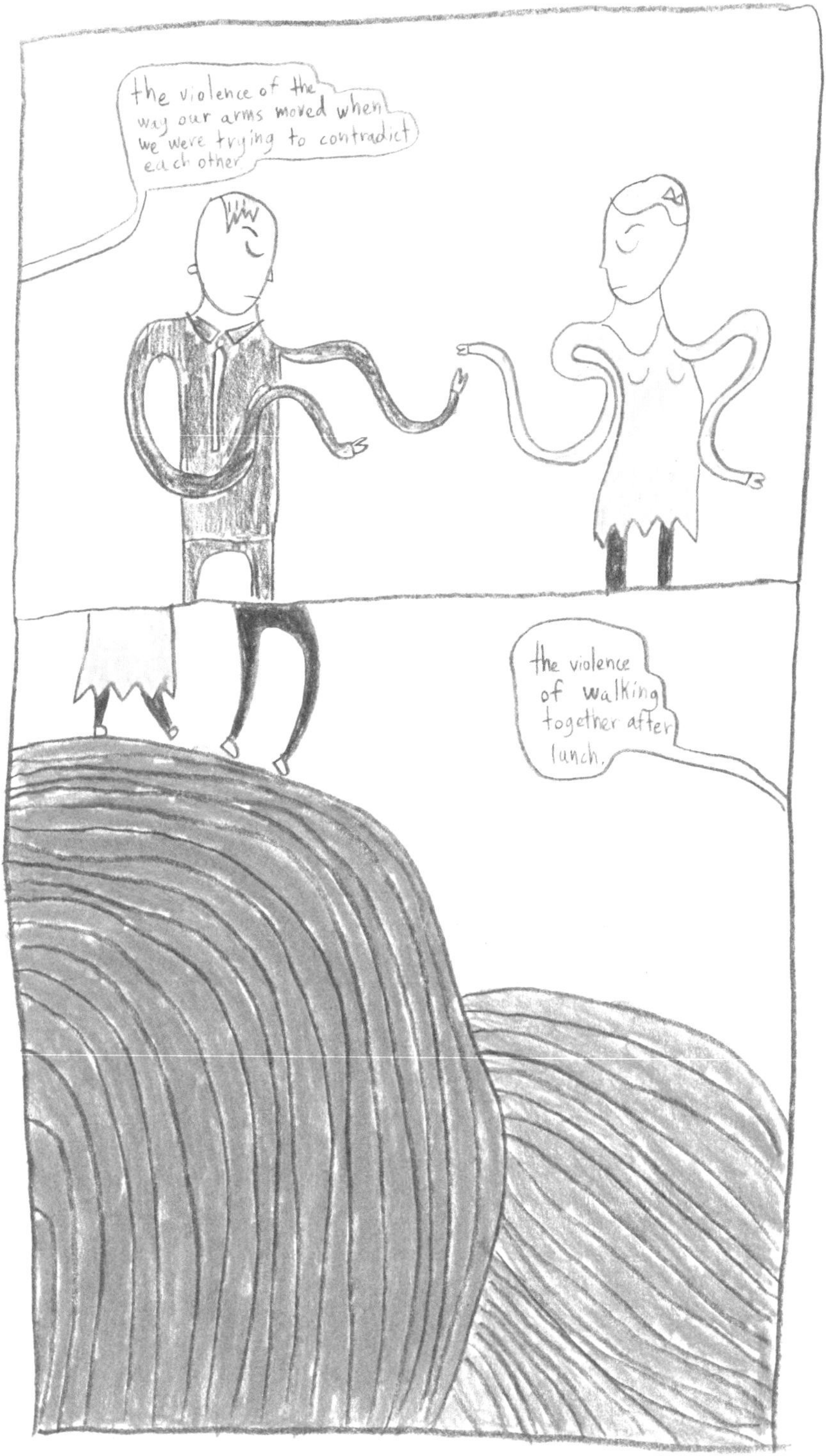
the violence of the way our arms moved when we were trying to contradict each other
the violence of walking together after lunch.

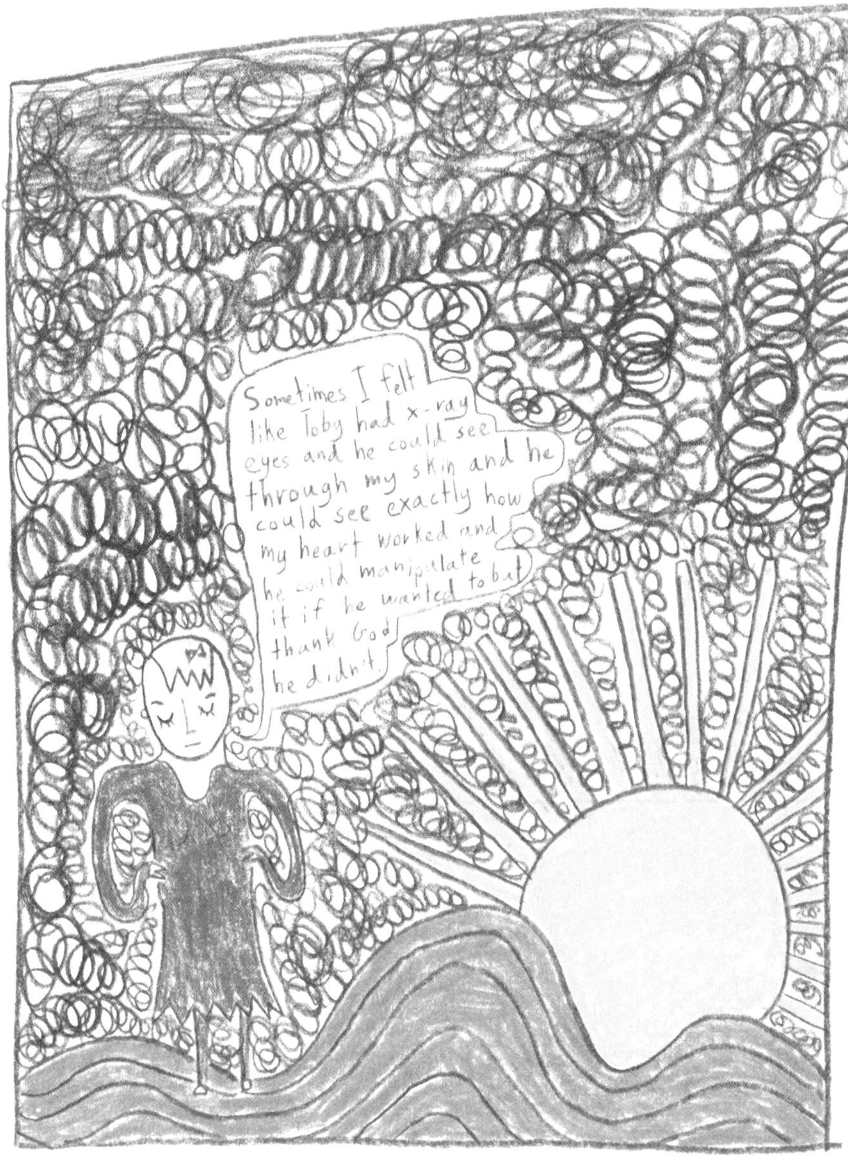
Sometimes I felt like Toby had x-ray eyes and he could see through my skin and he could see exactly how my heart worked and he could manipulate it if he wanted to but thank God he didn't.

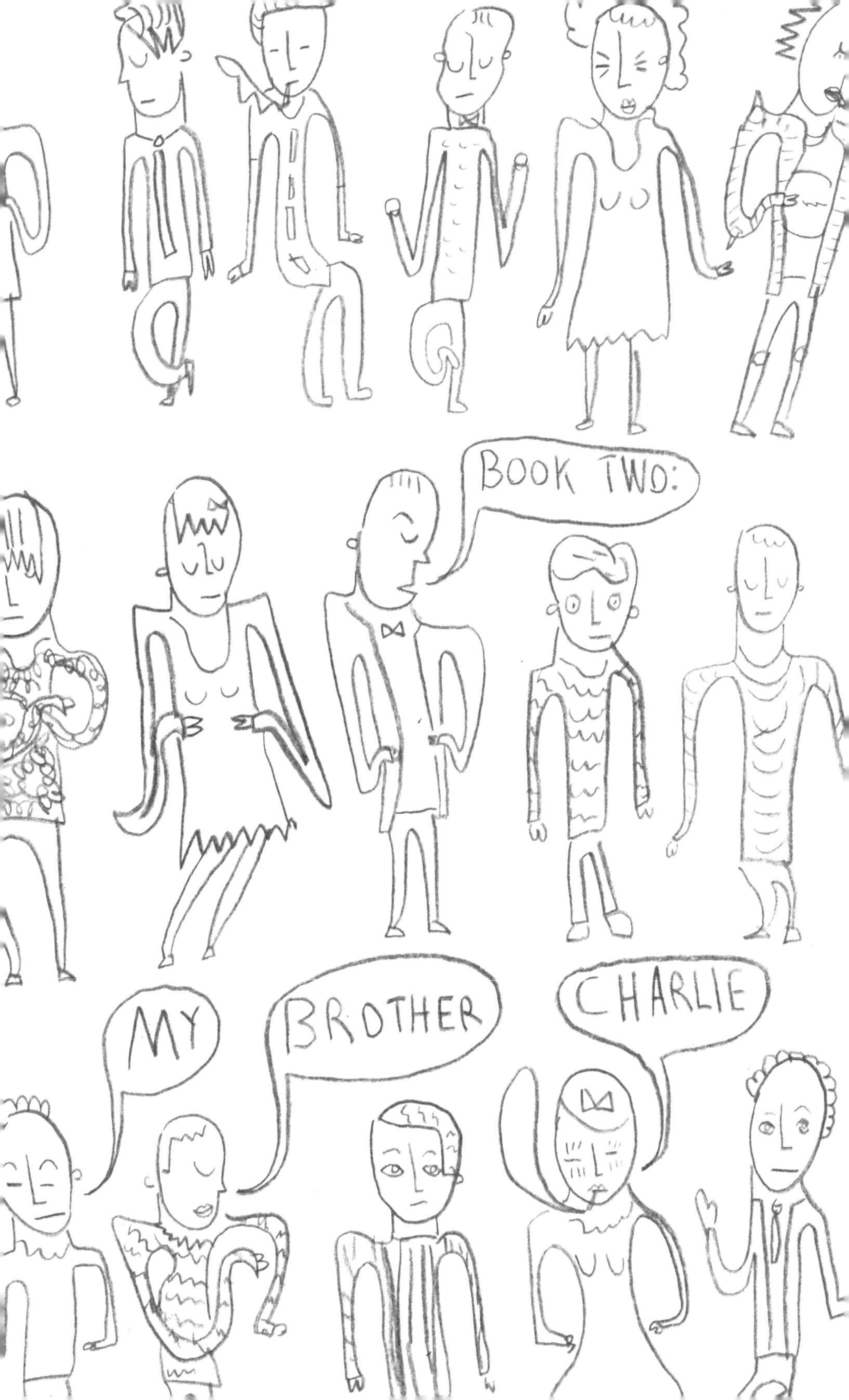
BOOK TWO:
MY
BROTHER
CHARLIE

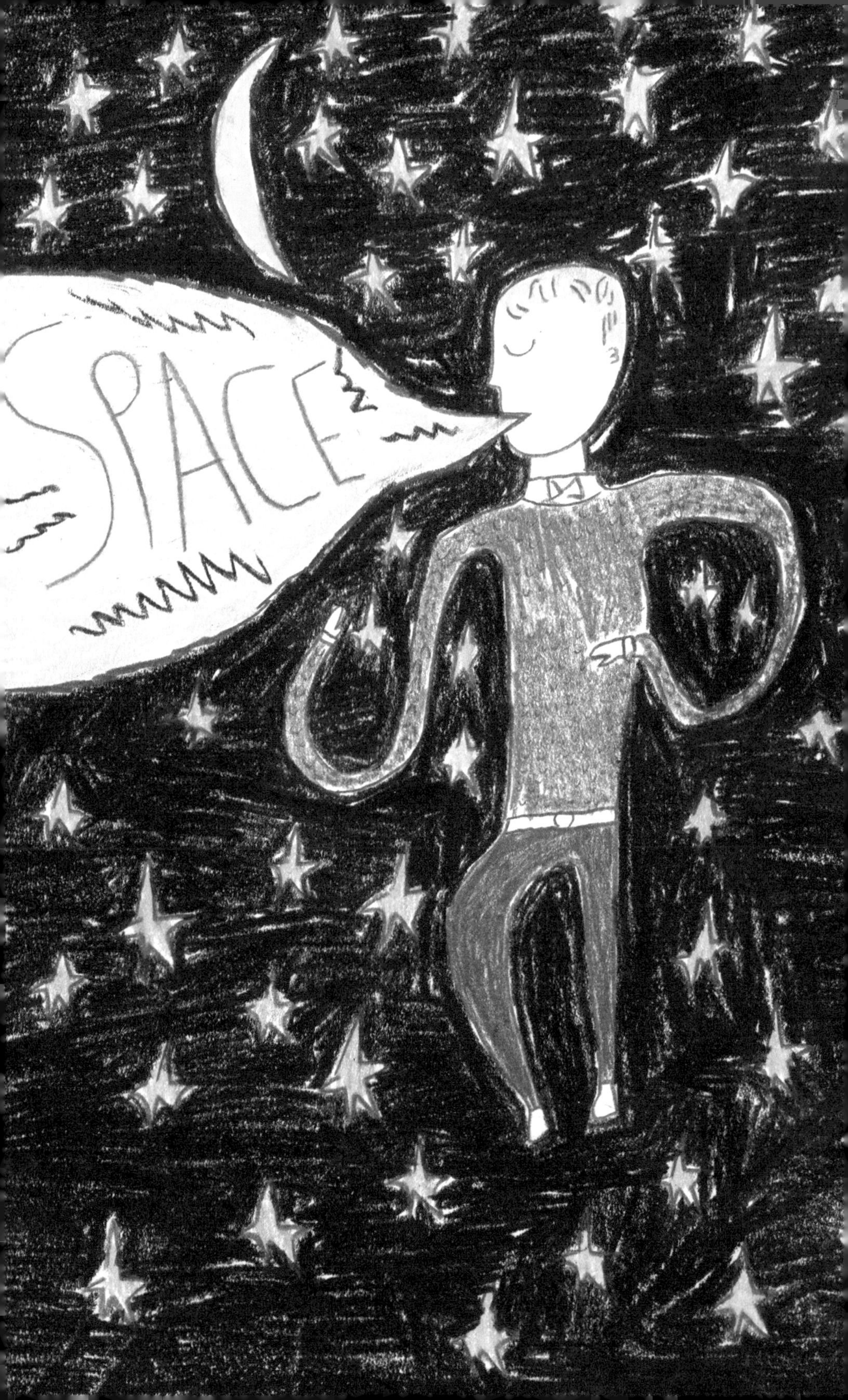
SPACE

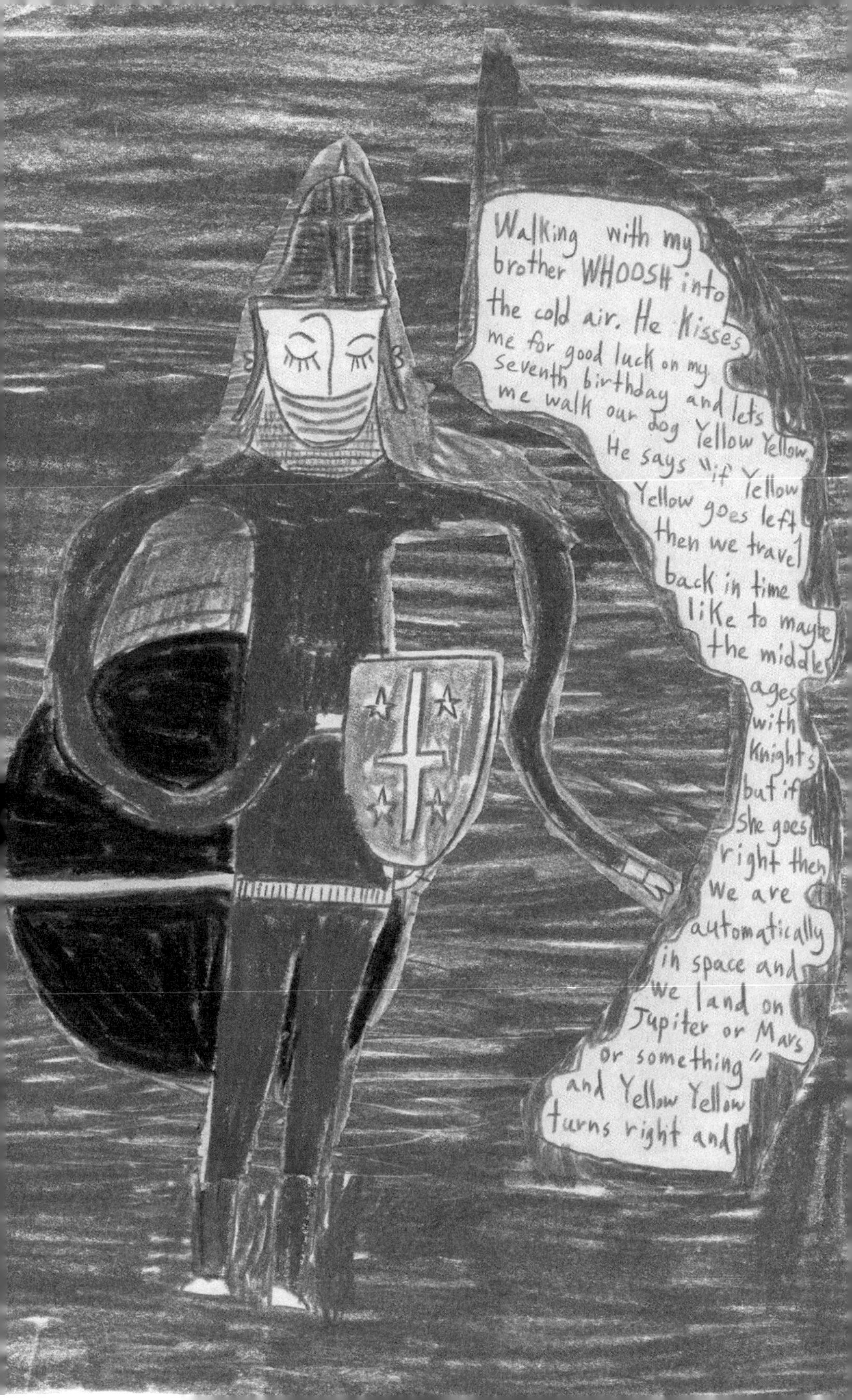
Walking with my brother WHOOSH into the cold air. He Kisses me for good luck on my Seventh birthday and lets me walk our dog Yellow Yellow. He says "if Yellow Yellow goes left then we travel back in time like to maybe the middle ages with Knights but if She goes right then we are automatically in space and we land on Jupiter or Mars or something" and Yellow Yellow turns right and

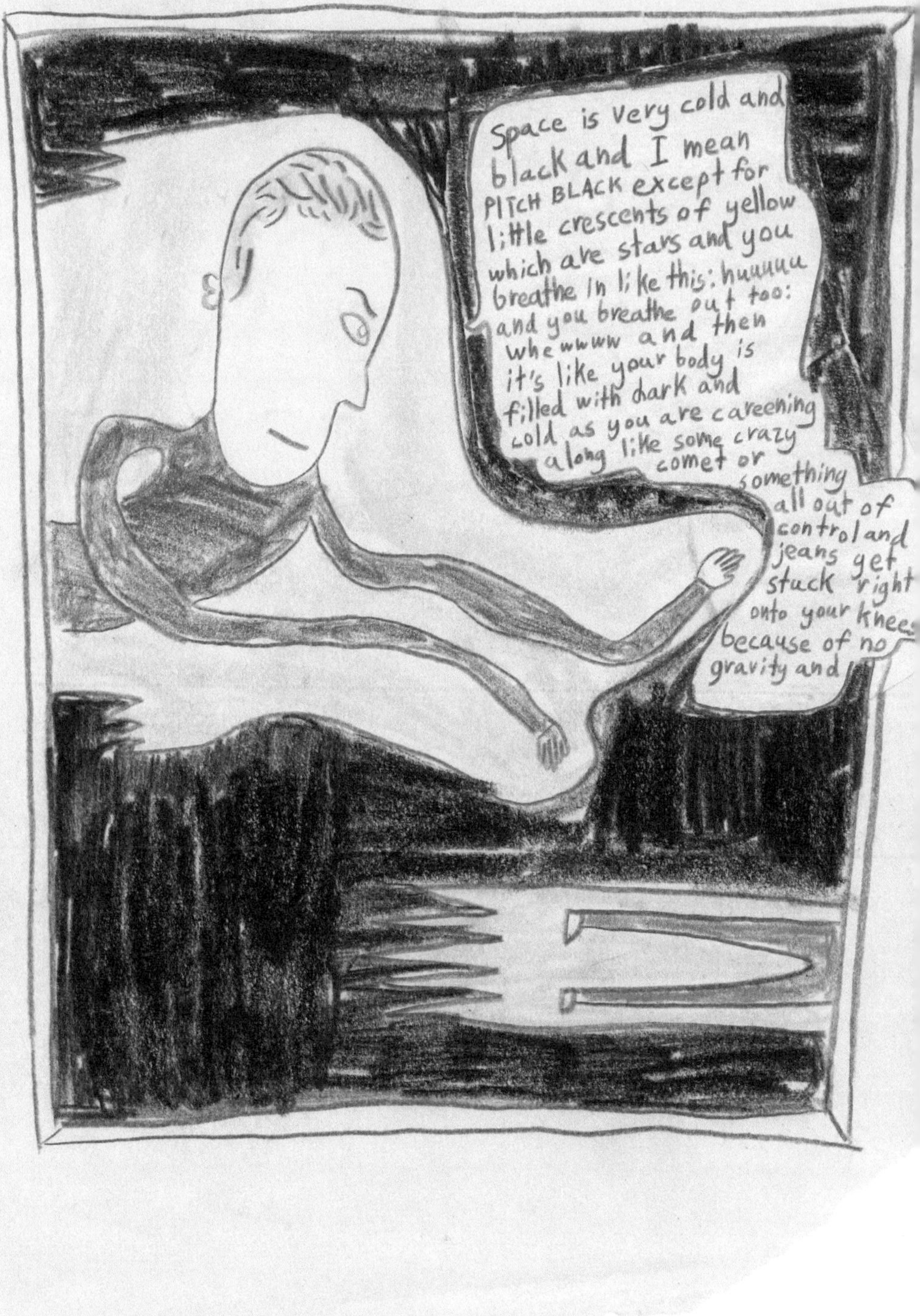
Space is very cold and black and I mean PITCH BLACK except for little crescents of yellow which are stars and you breathe in like this: huuuuu and you breathe out too: whewwww and then it's like your body is filled with dark and cold as you are careening along like some crazy comet or
something all out of control and jeans get stuck right onto your knees because of no gravity and

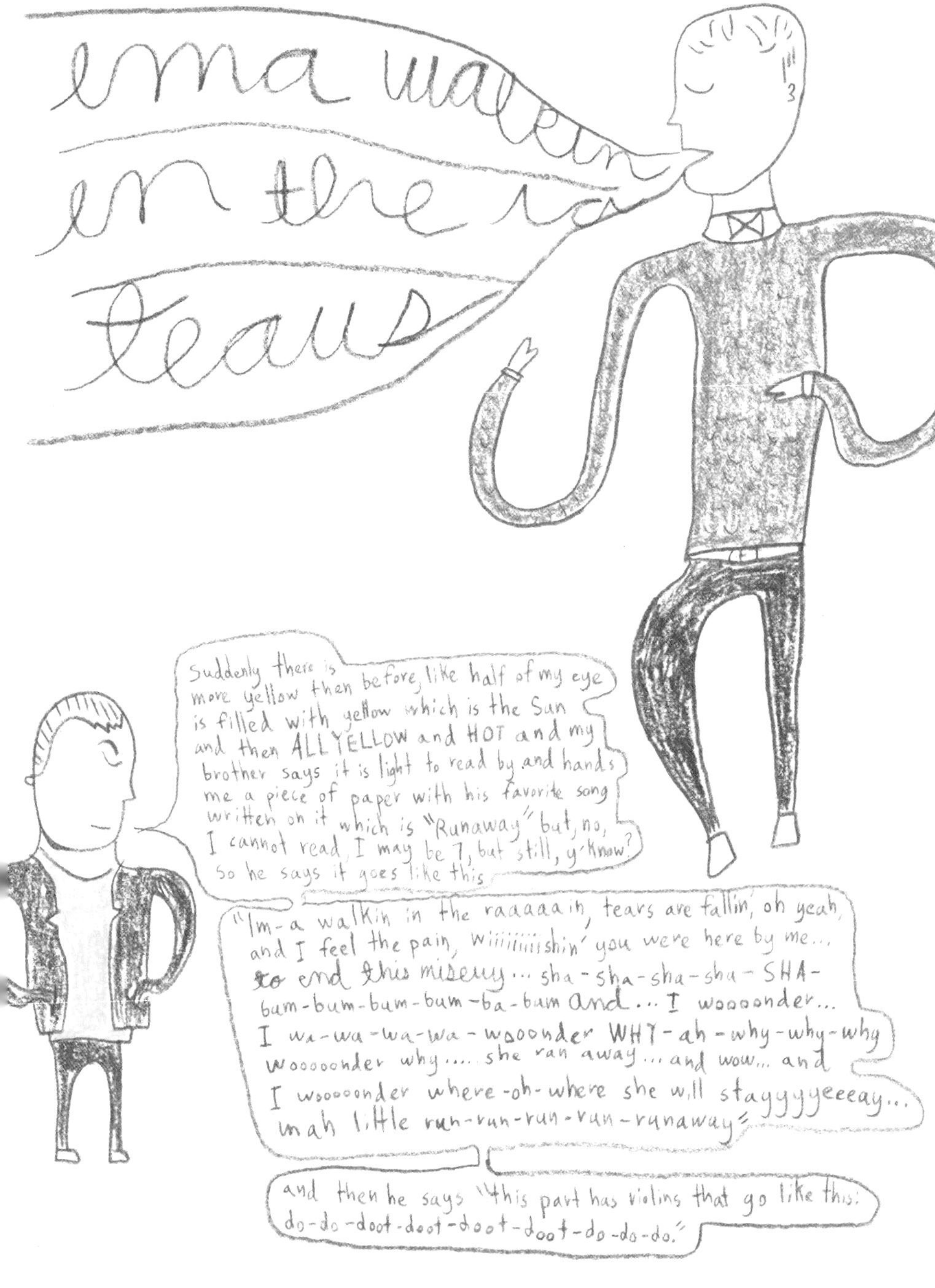
ima walkin
in the ra
tears
Suddenly there is more yellow then before, like half of my eye is filled with yellow which is the Sun and then ALL YELLOW and HOT and my brother says it is light to read by and hands me a piece of paper with his favorite song written on it which is "Runaway" but, no, I cannot read, I may be 7, but still, y'know? So he says it goes like this
"Im-a walkin in the raaaaain, tears are fallin', oh yeah, and I feel the pain, wiiiiiiiiishin' you were here by me... to end this misery... sha-sha-sha-sha-SHA-bum-bum-bum-bum-ba-bum and... I woooonder... I wa-wa-wa-wa-wooonder WHY-ah-why-why-why woooooonder why.... she ran away... and wow... and I woooooonder where-oh-where she will stayyyyeeeay... mah little run-run-run-run-runaway"
and then he says "this part has violins that go like this: do-do-doot-doot-doot-doot-do-do-do."

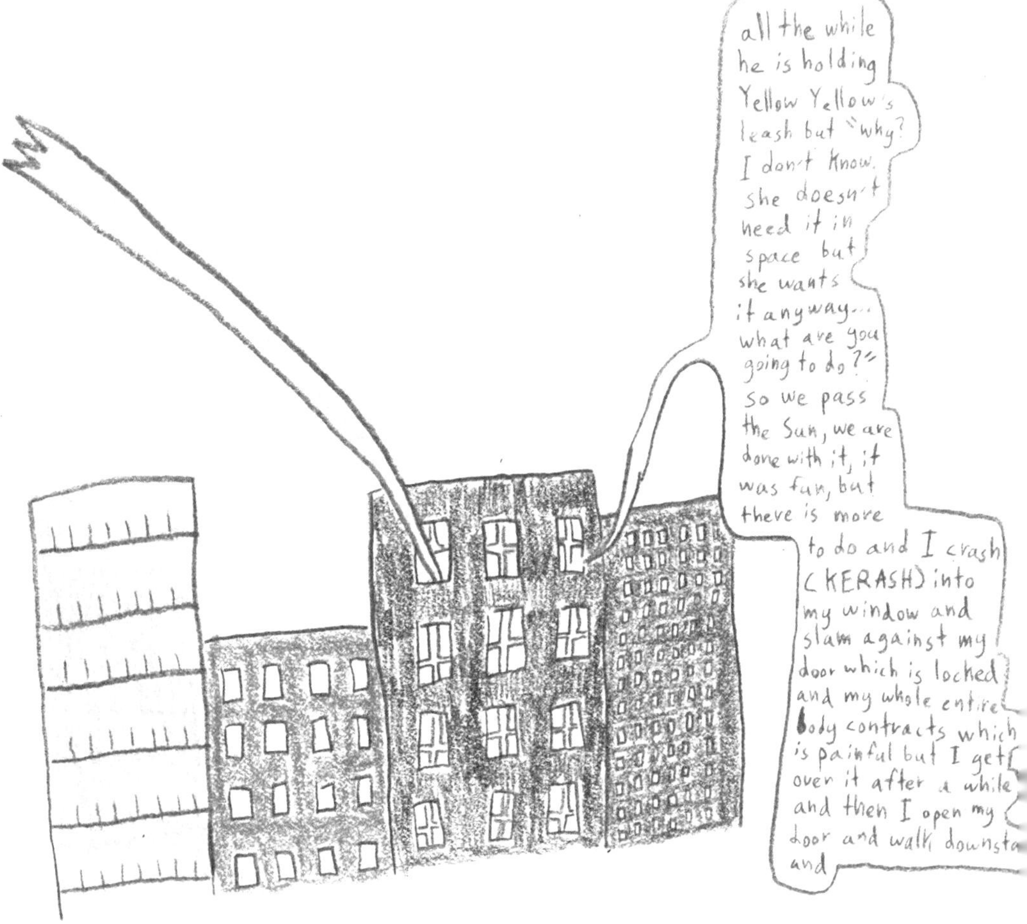
all the while he is holding Yellow Yellow's leash but "why? I don't know. she doesn't need it in space but she wants it anyway... what are you going to do?" so we pass the Sun, we are done with it, it was fun, but there is more to do and I crash (KERASH) into my window and slam against my door which is locked and my whole entire body contracts which is painful but I get over it after a while and then I open my door and walk downsta and

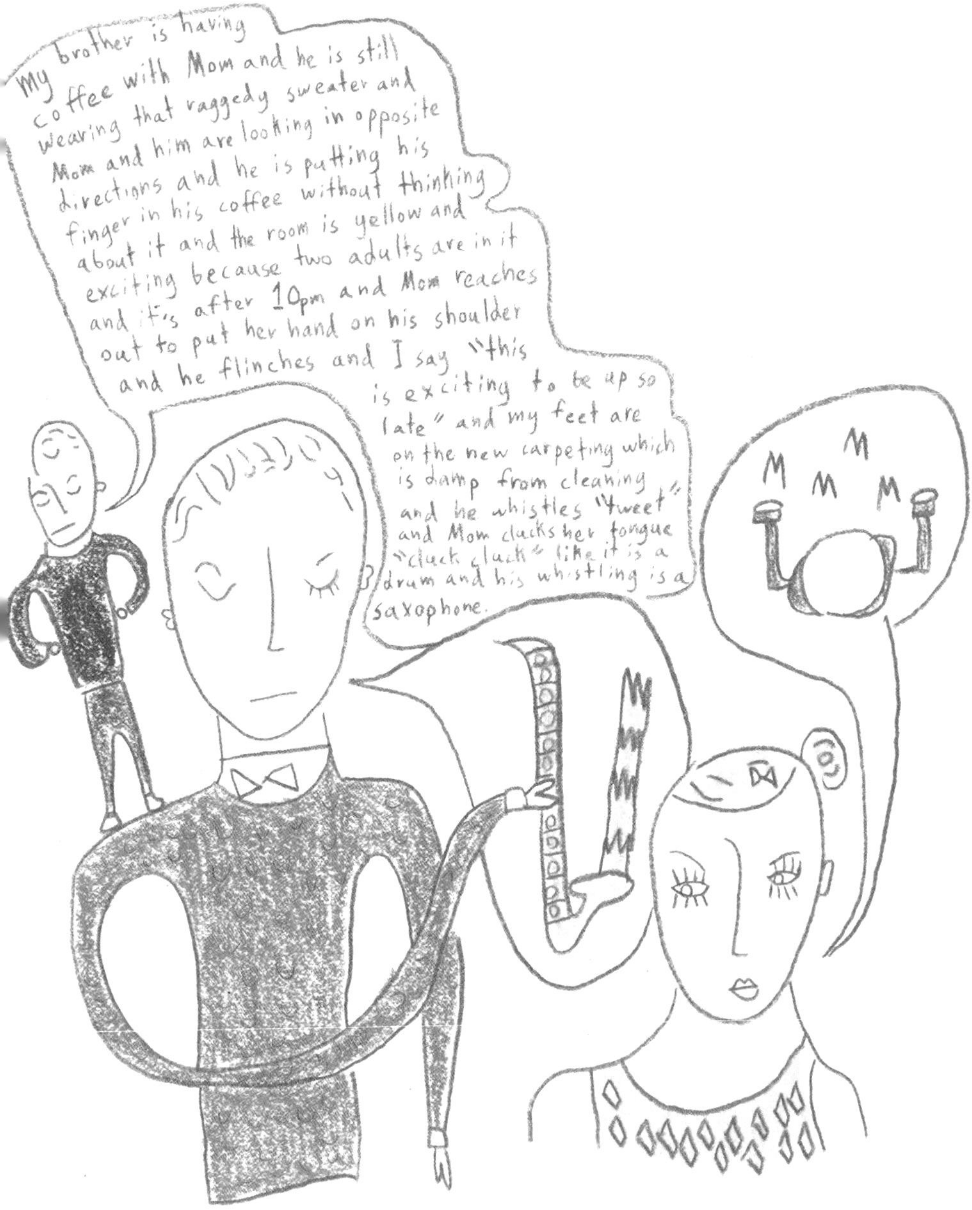
My brother is having coffee with Mom and he is still wearing that raggedy sweater and Mom and him are looking in opposite directions and he is putting his finger in his coffee without thinking about it and the room is yellow and exciting because two adults are in it and it's after 10pm and Mom reaches out to put her hand on his shoulder and he flinches and I say "this is exciting to be up so late" and my feet are on the new carpeting which is damp from cleaning and he whistles "tweet" and Mom clucks her tongue "cluck cluck" like it is a drum and his whistling is a saxophone.
M M M M

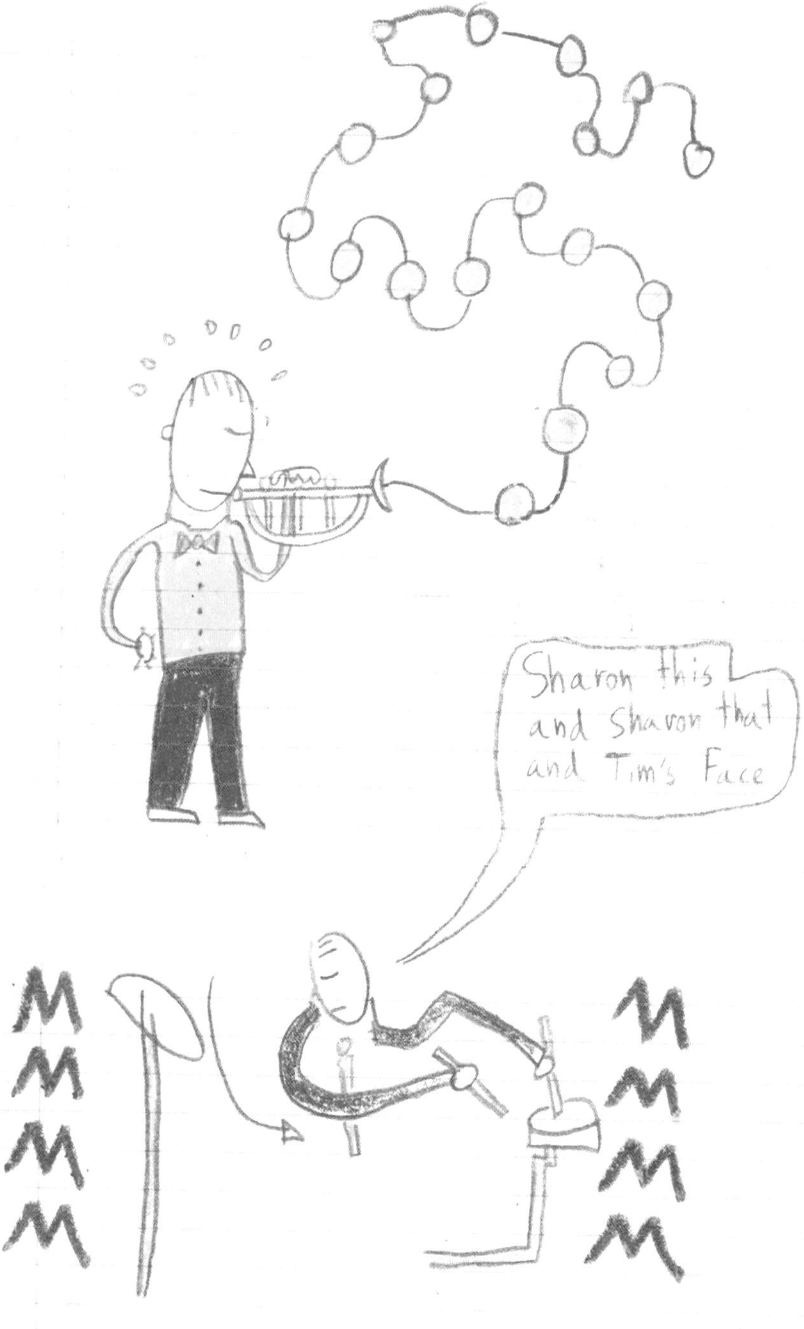
Sharon this and Sharon that and Tim's Face

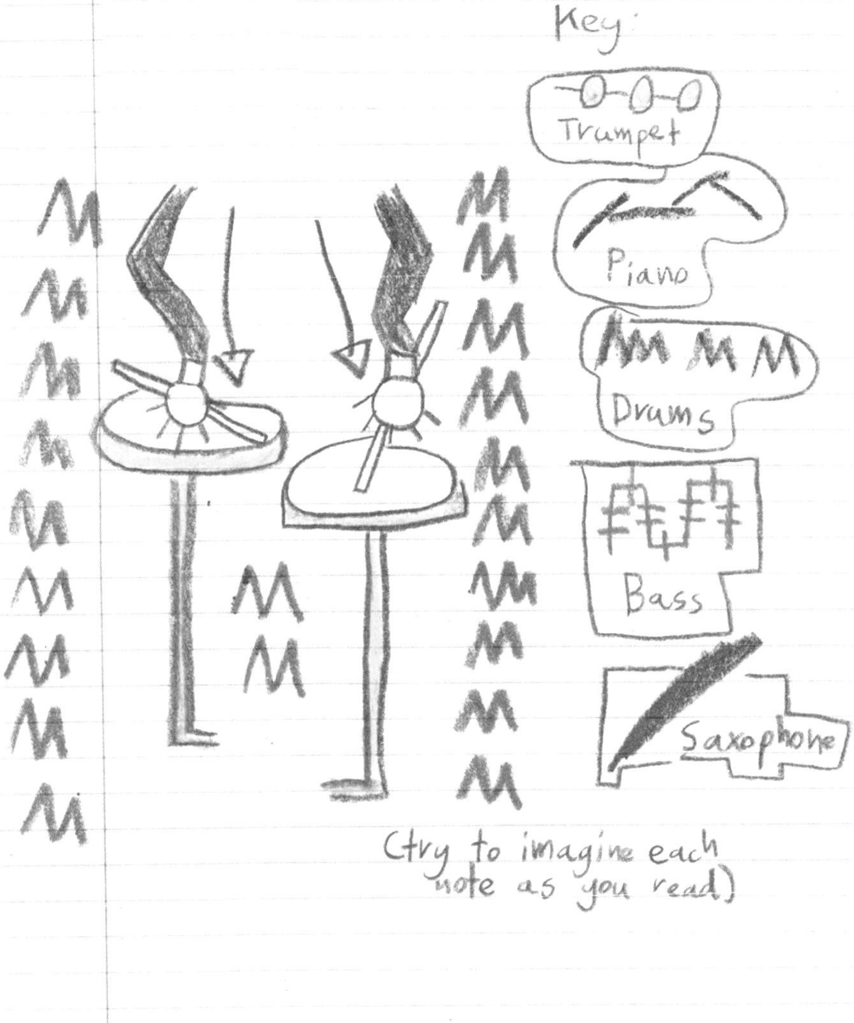
Key:
Trumpet
Piano
Drums
Bass
Saxophone

(try to imagine each note as you read)

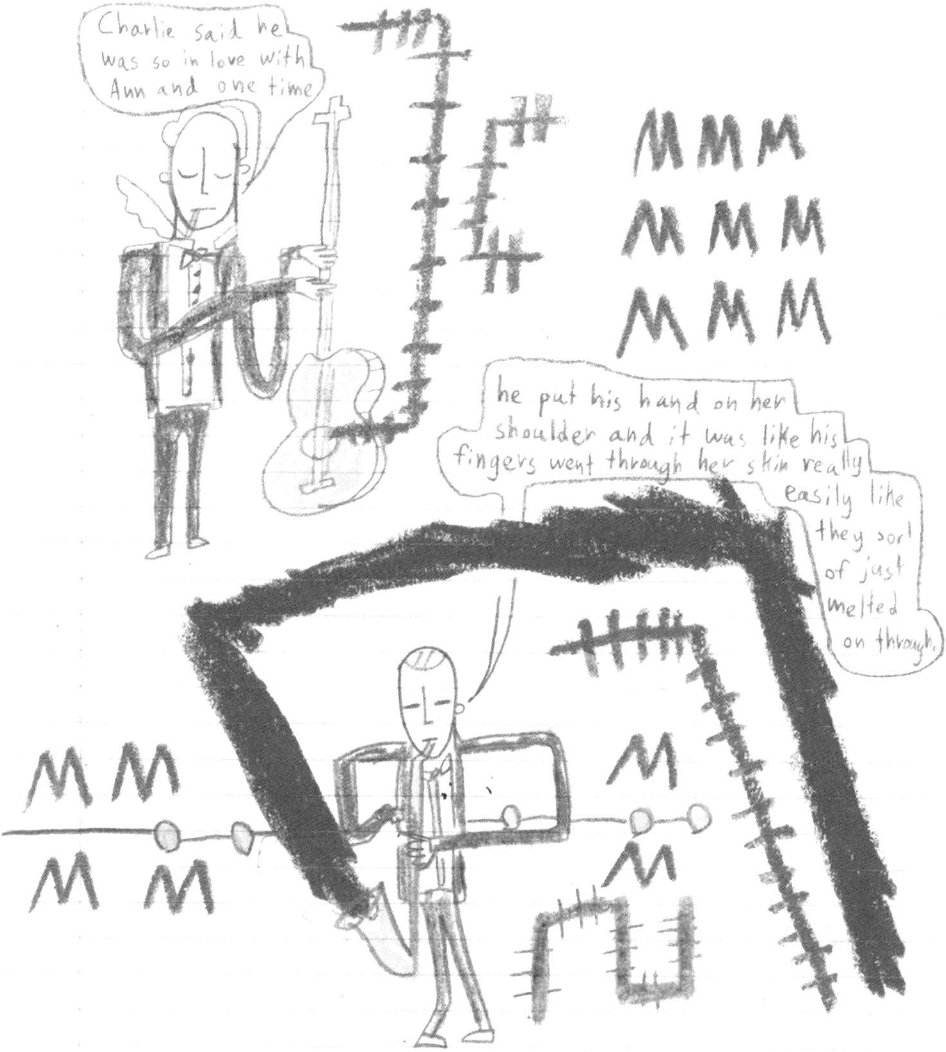
Charlie said he was so in love with Ann and one time
he put his hand on her shoulder and it was like his fingers went through her skin really easily like they sort of just melted on through.

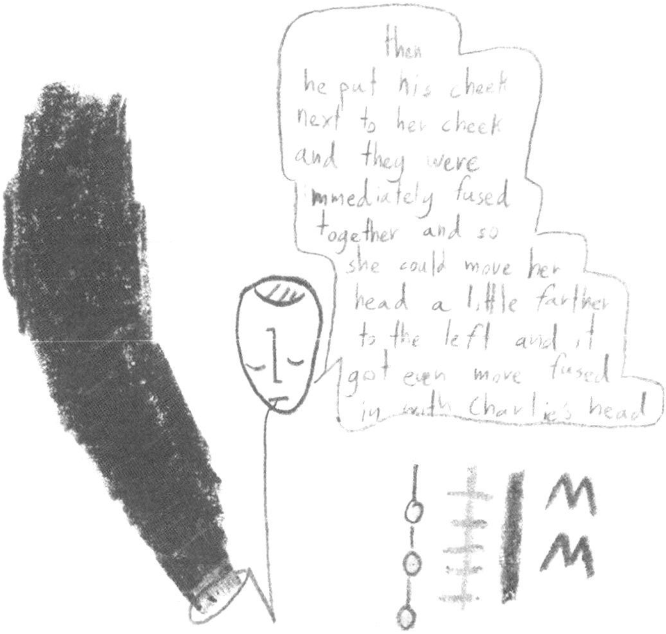
then
he put his cheek
next to her cheek
and they were
immediately fused
together and so
she could move her
head a little farther
to the left and it
got even more fused
in with Charlie's head

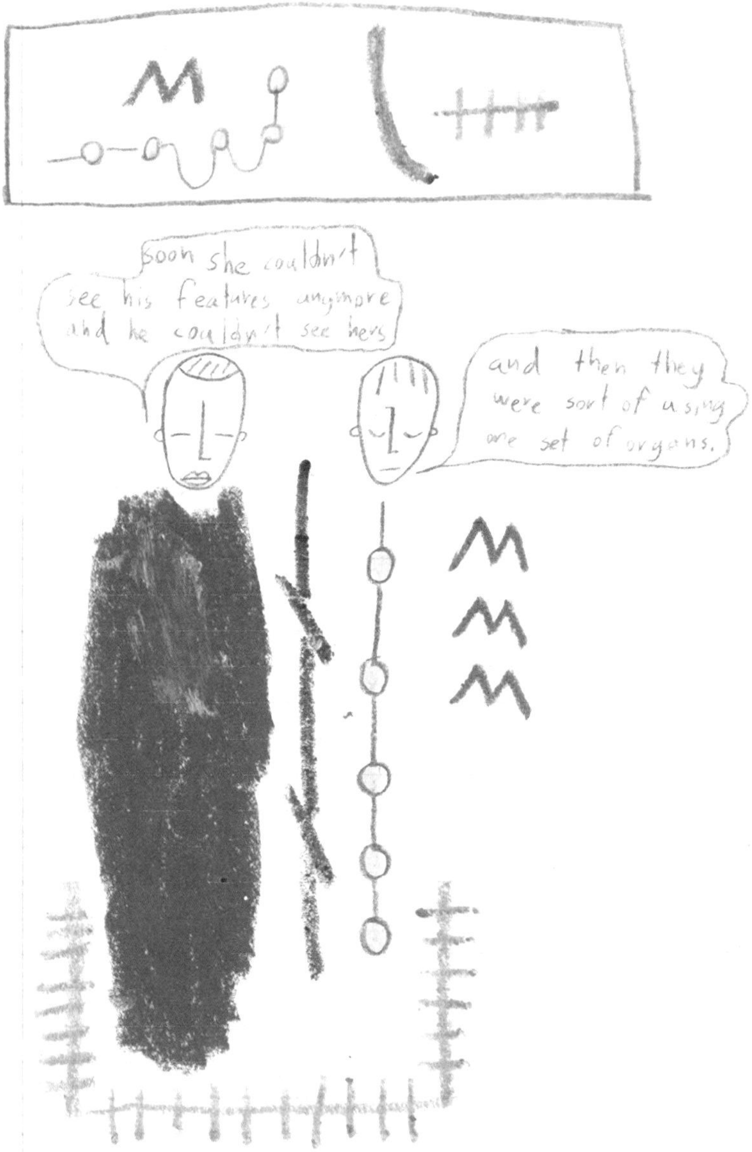
Soon she couldn't see his features anymore and he couldn't see hers
and then they were sort of using one set of organs.

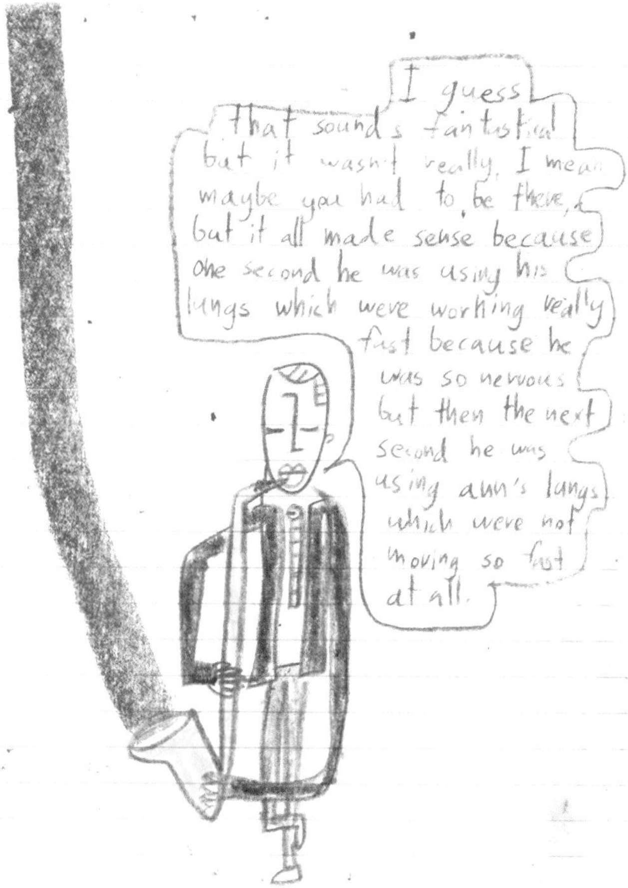
I guess that sounds fantastical but it wasn't really. I mean maybe you had to be there, but it all made sense because one second he was using his lungs which were working really fast because he was so nervous but then the next second he was using ann's lungs which were not moving so fast at all.

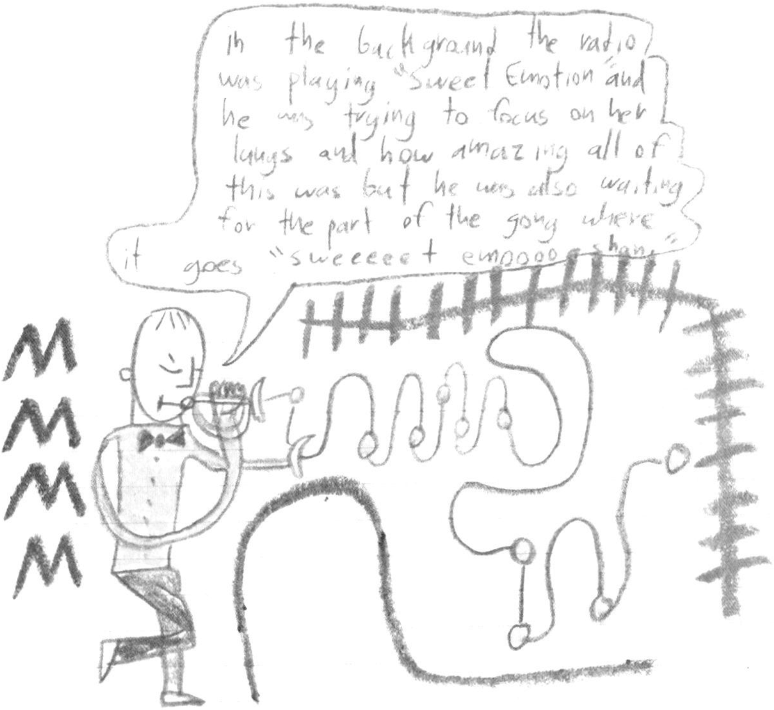
In the backgraund the radio was playing "Sweet Emotion" and he was trying to focus on her lungs and how amazing all of this was but he was also waiting for the part of the gong where it goes "sweeeeeet emoooo shan."
M
M
M
M

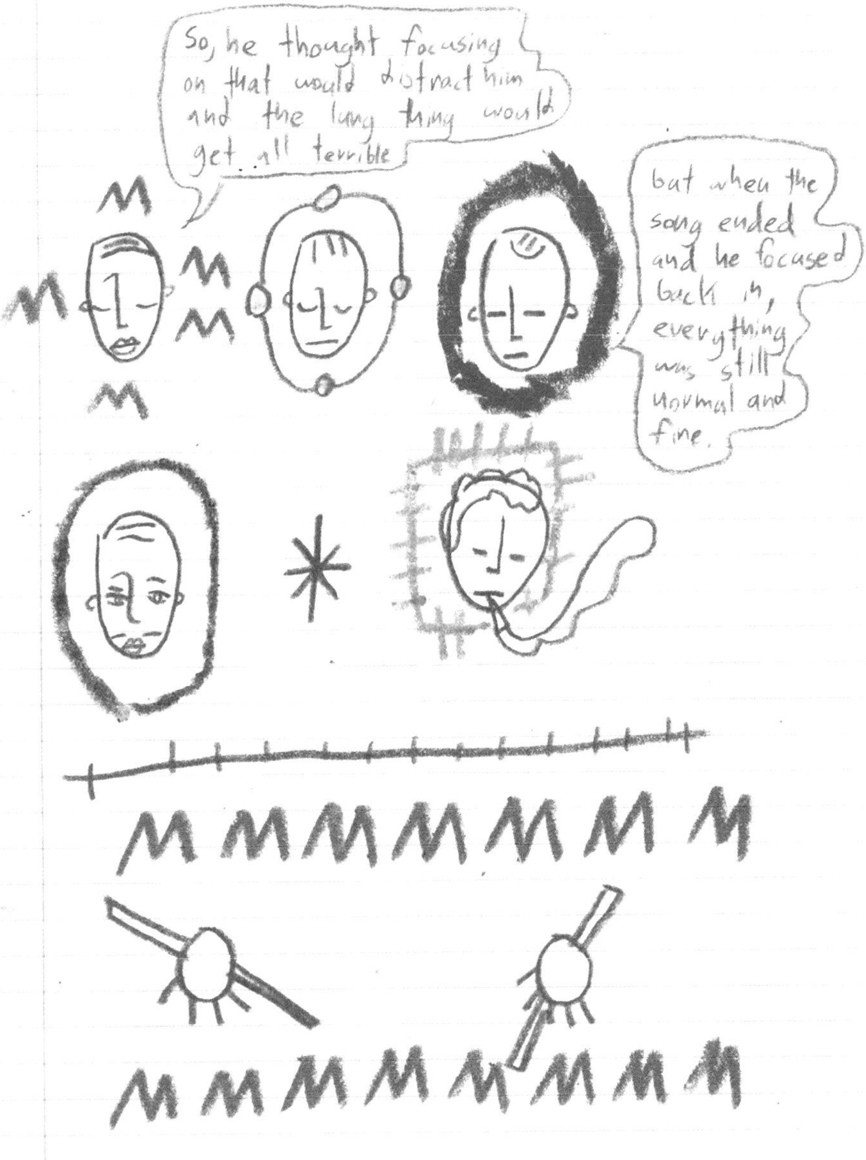
So, he thought focusing on that would distract him and the long thing would get all terrible
but when the song ended and he focused back in, everything was still normal and fine.

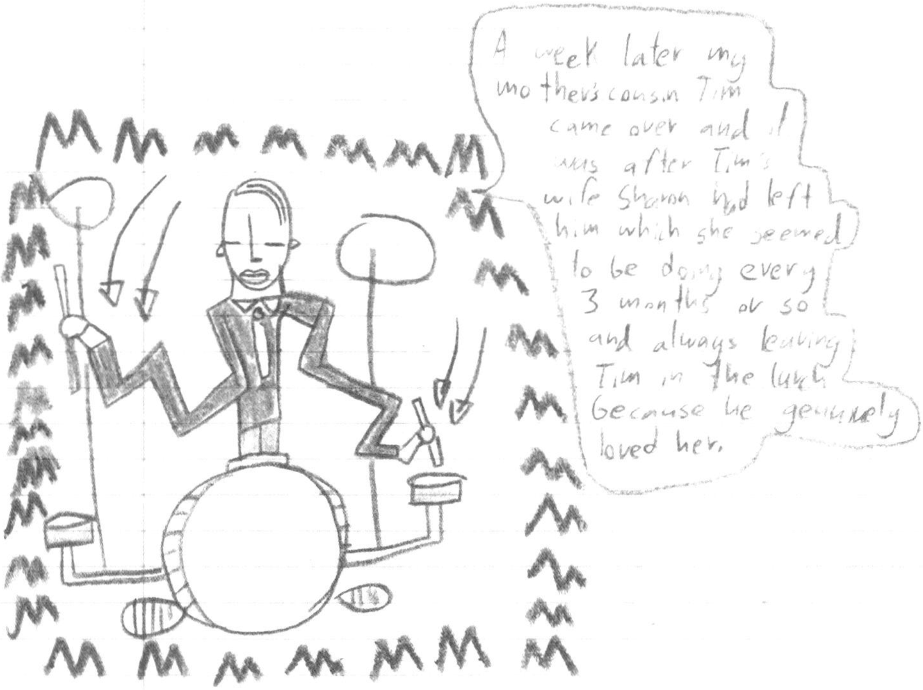
A week later my mother's cousin Tim came over and it was after Tim's wife Sharon had left him which she seemed to be doing every 3 months or so and always leaving Tim in the lurch because he genuinely loved her.

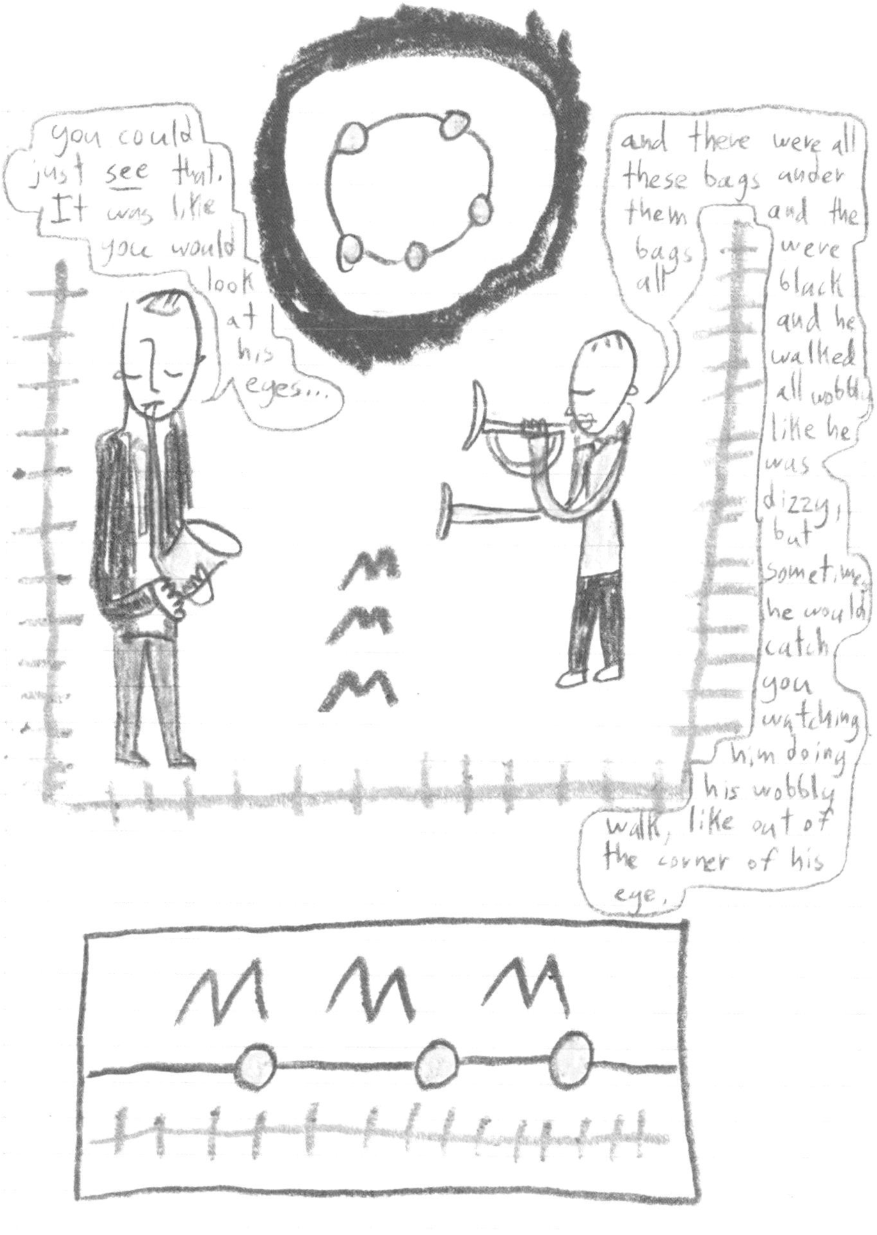

you could just see that. It was like you would look at his eyes...
and there were all these bags under them and the bags all were black and he walked all wobbly like he was dizzy, but sometimes he would catch you watching him doing his wobbly walk, like out of the corner of his eye.
MMM
MMM

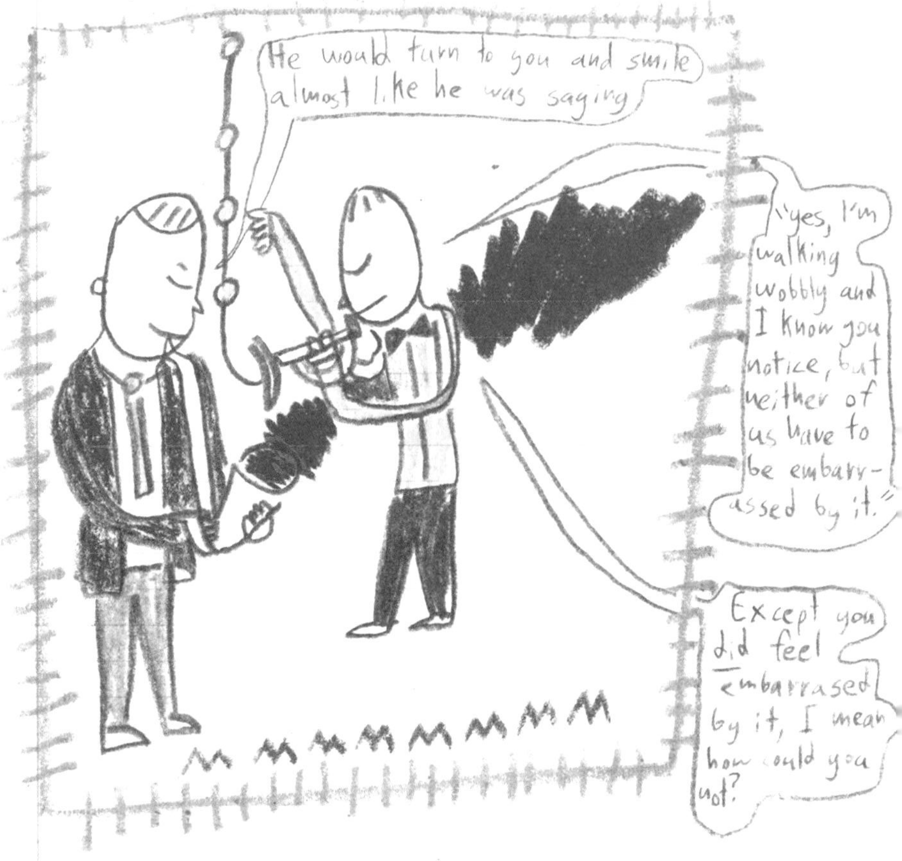
He would turn to you and smile almost like he was saying
"yes, I'm walking wobbly and I know you notice, but neither of us have to be embarrassed by it."
Except you did feel embarrased by it, I mean how could you not?

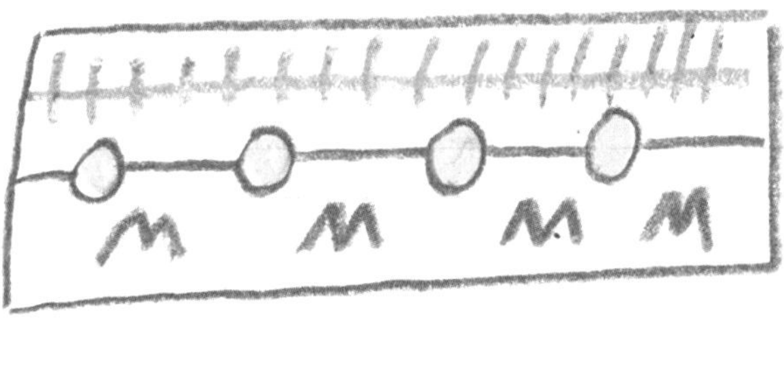

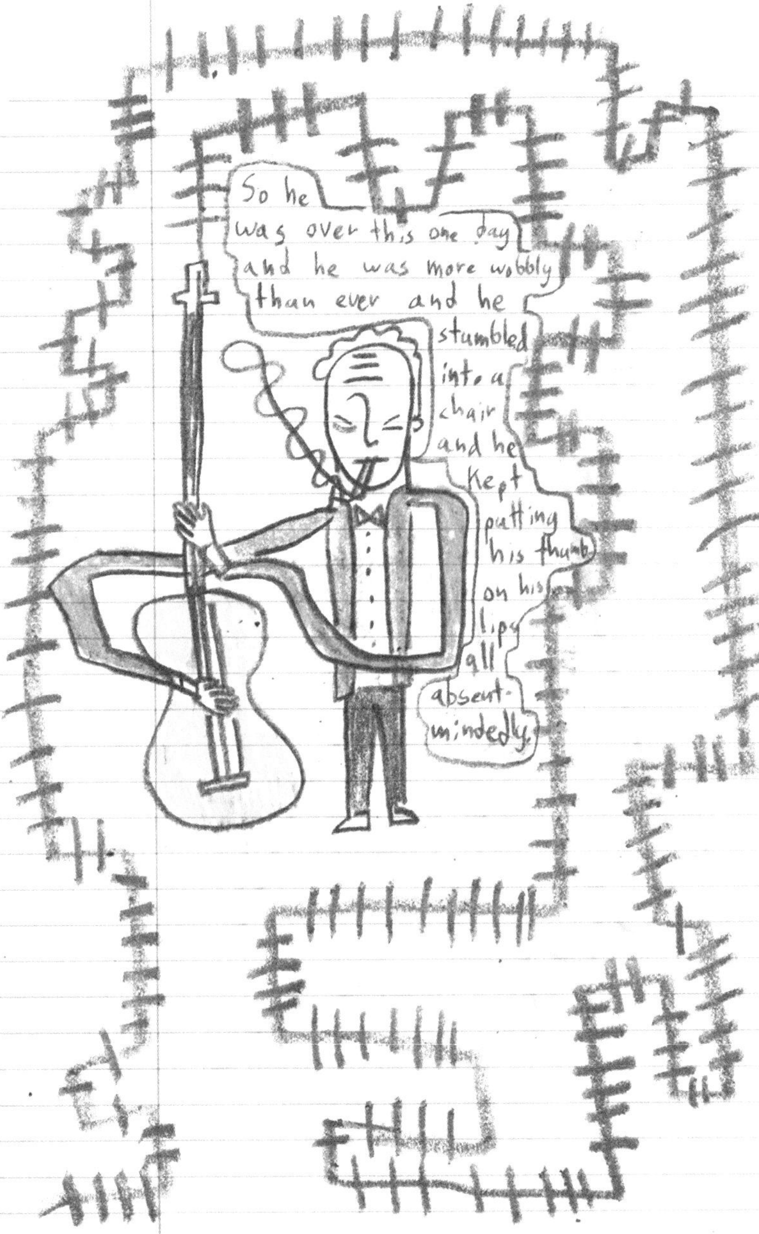
So he was over this one day and he was more wobbly than ever and he stumbled into a chair and he kept putting his thumb on his lips all absent-mindedly.

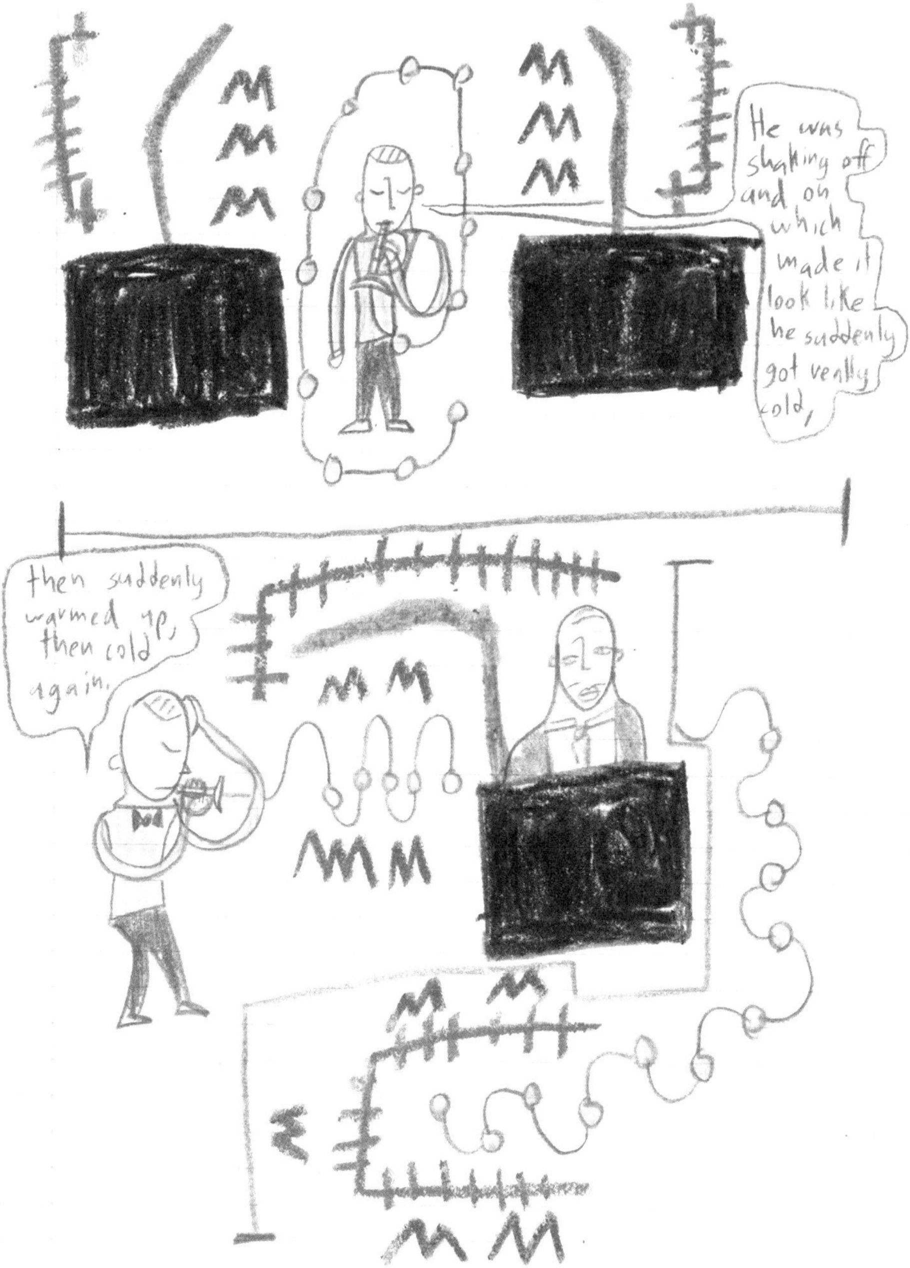
He was shaking off and on which made it look like he suddenly got really cold,
then suddenly warmed up, then cold again.

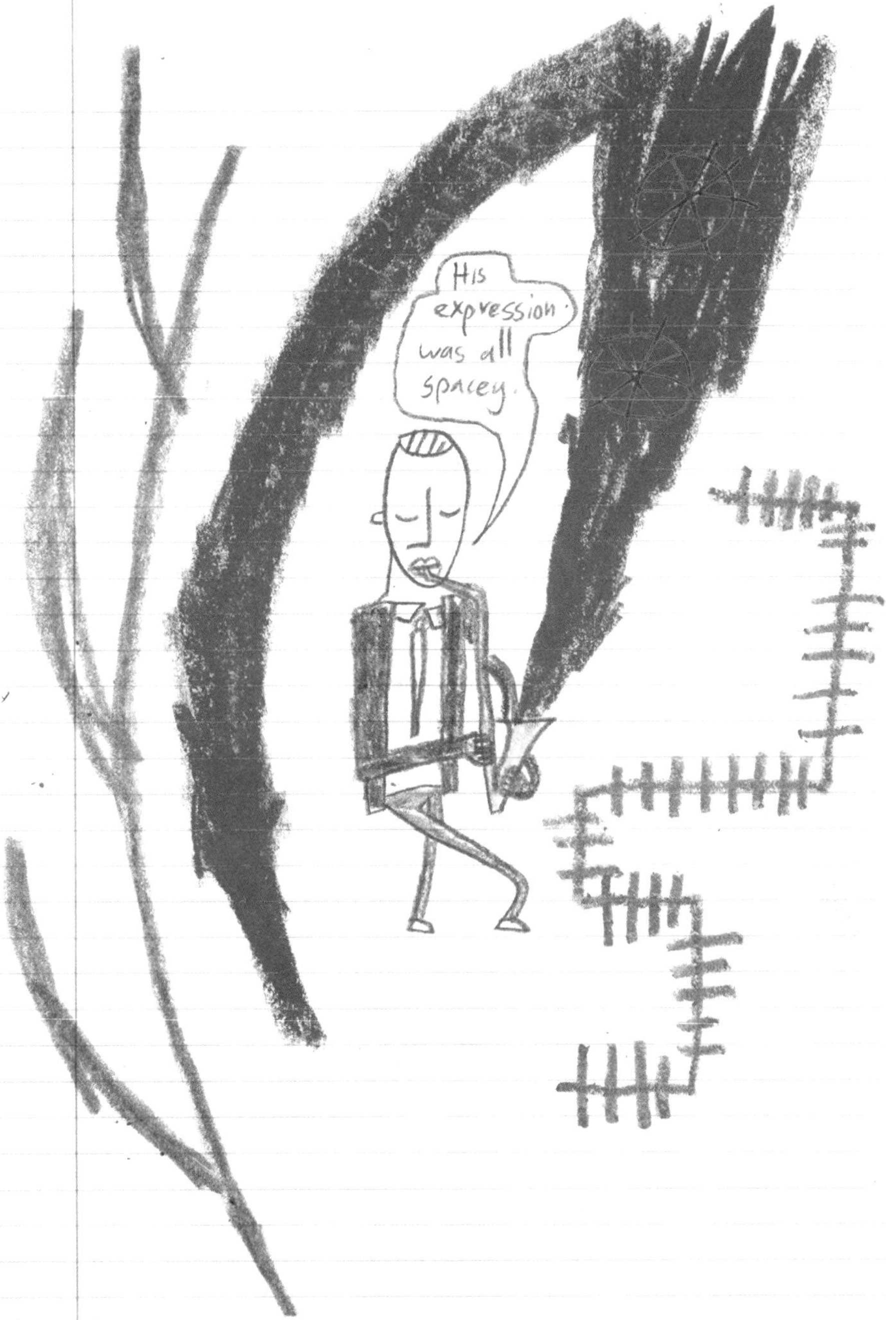
His expression was all spacey.

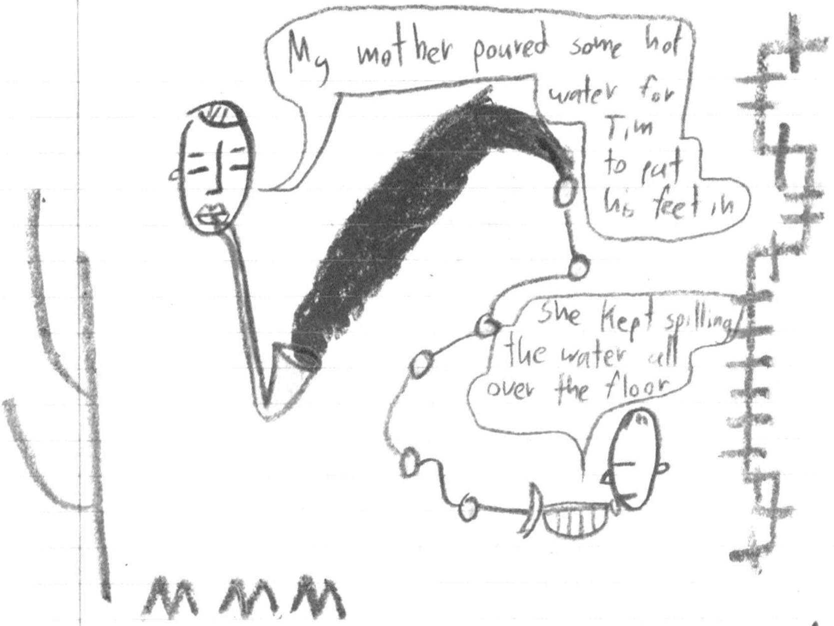
My mother poured some hot water for Tim to put his feet in
She kept spilling the water all over the floor

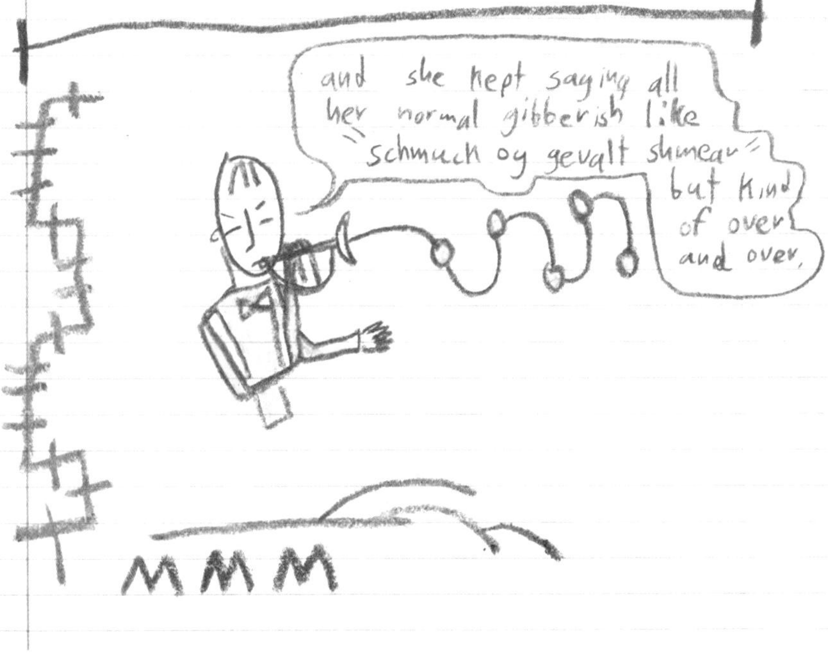
and she kept saying all her normal gibberish like "schmuck oy gevalt shmear" but kind of over and over,

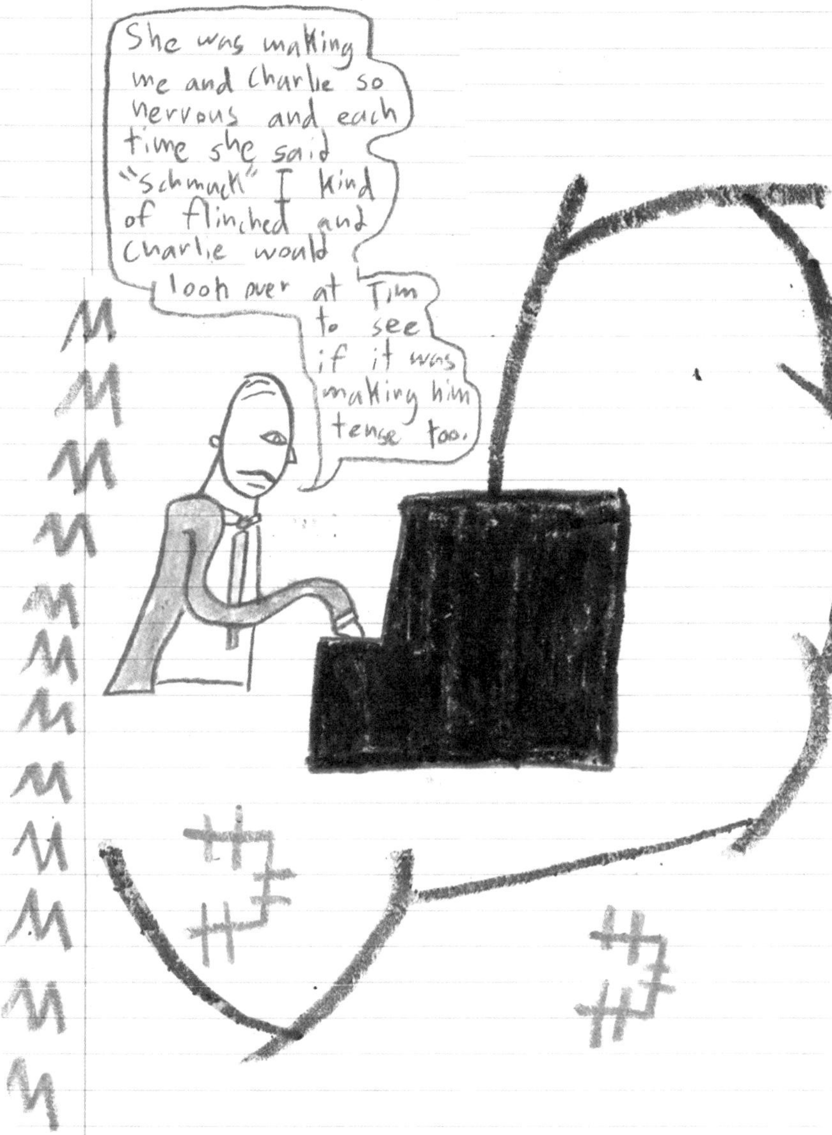
She was making me and Charlie so nervous and each time she said "schmuck" I kind of flinched and Charlie would look over at Tim to see if it was making him tense too.

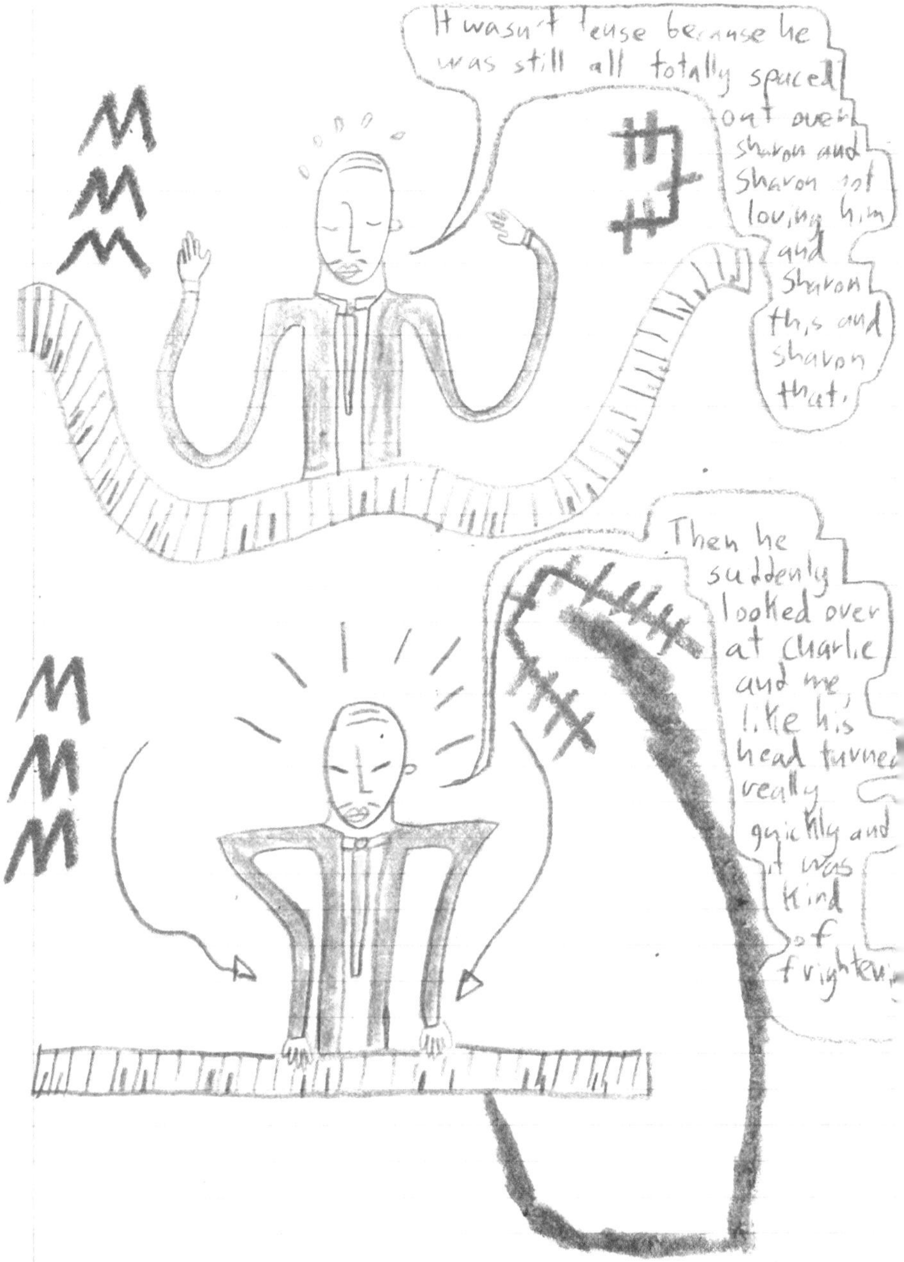
It wasn't tense because he was still all totally spaced out over Sharon and Sharon got loving him and Sharon this and Sharon that.
Then he suddenly looked over at Charlie and me, like his head turned really quickly and it was kind of frighteni

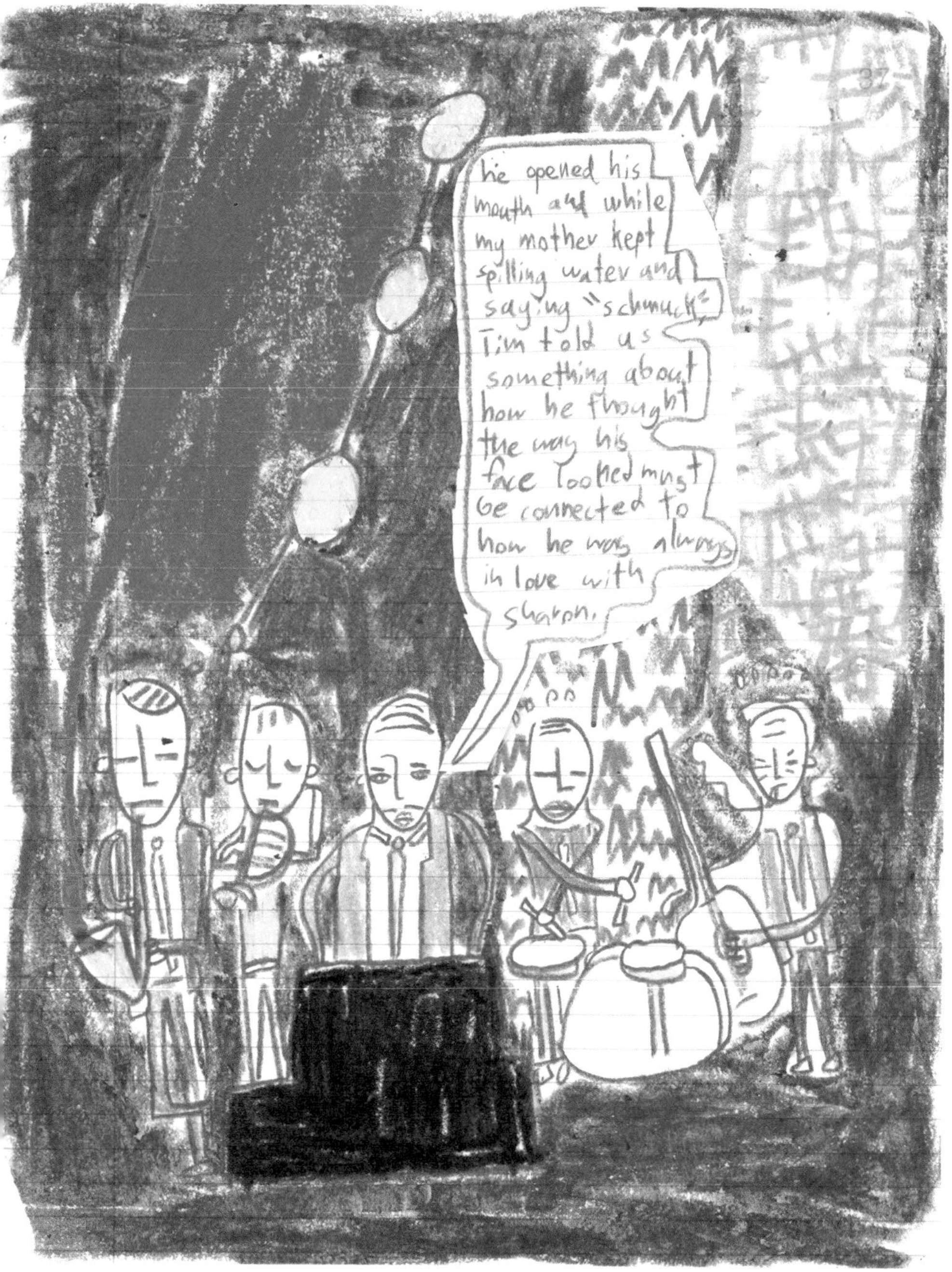
he opened his mouth and while my mother kept spilling water and saying "schmuck," Tim told us something about how he thought the way his face looked must be connected to how he was always in love with sharon.

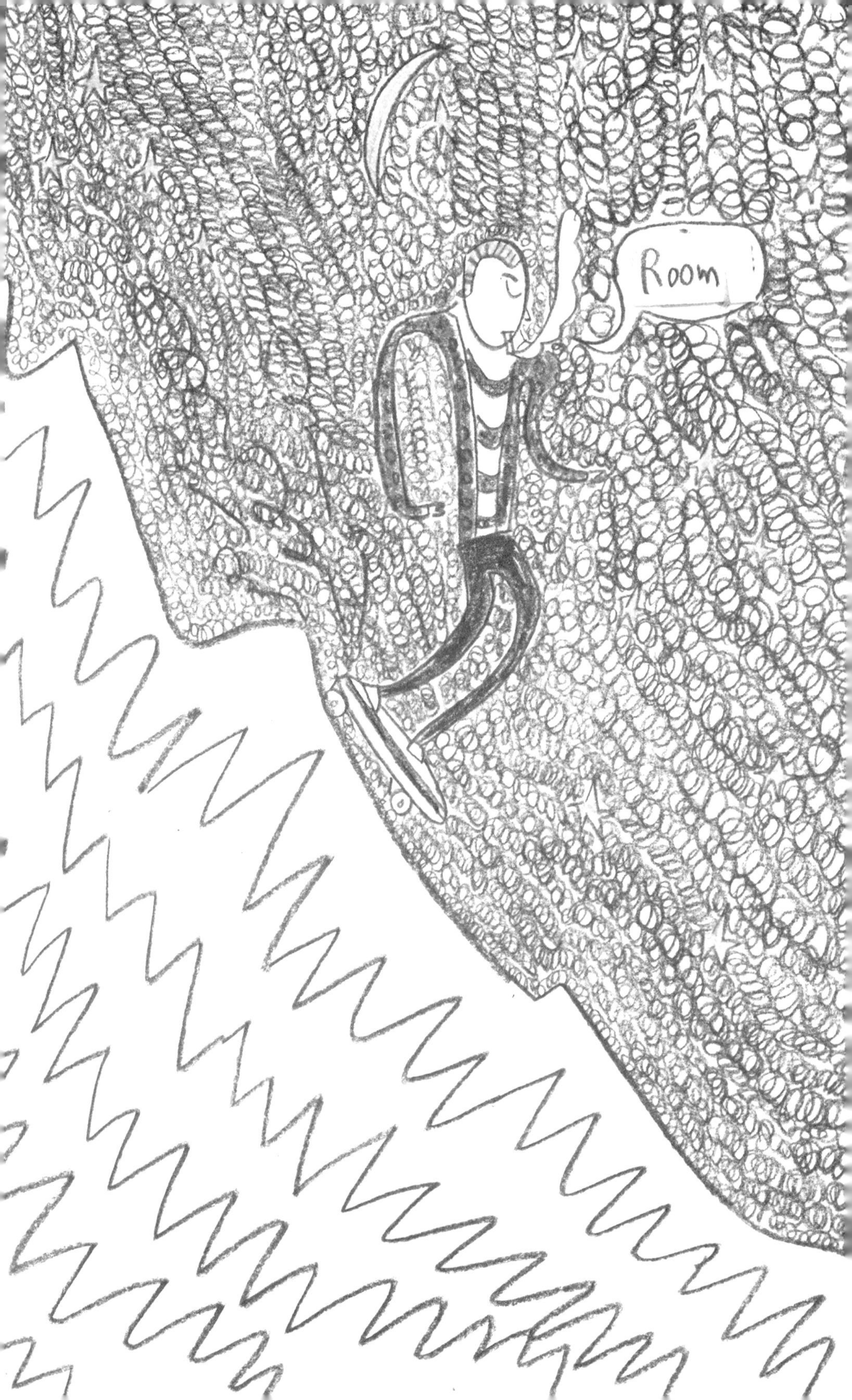
Room

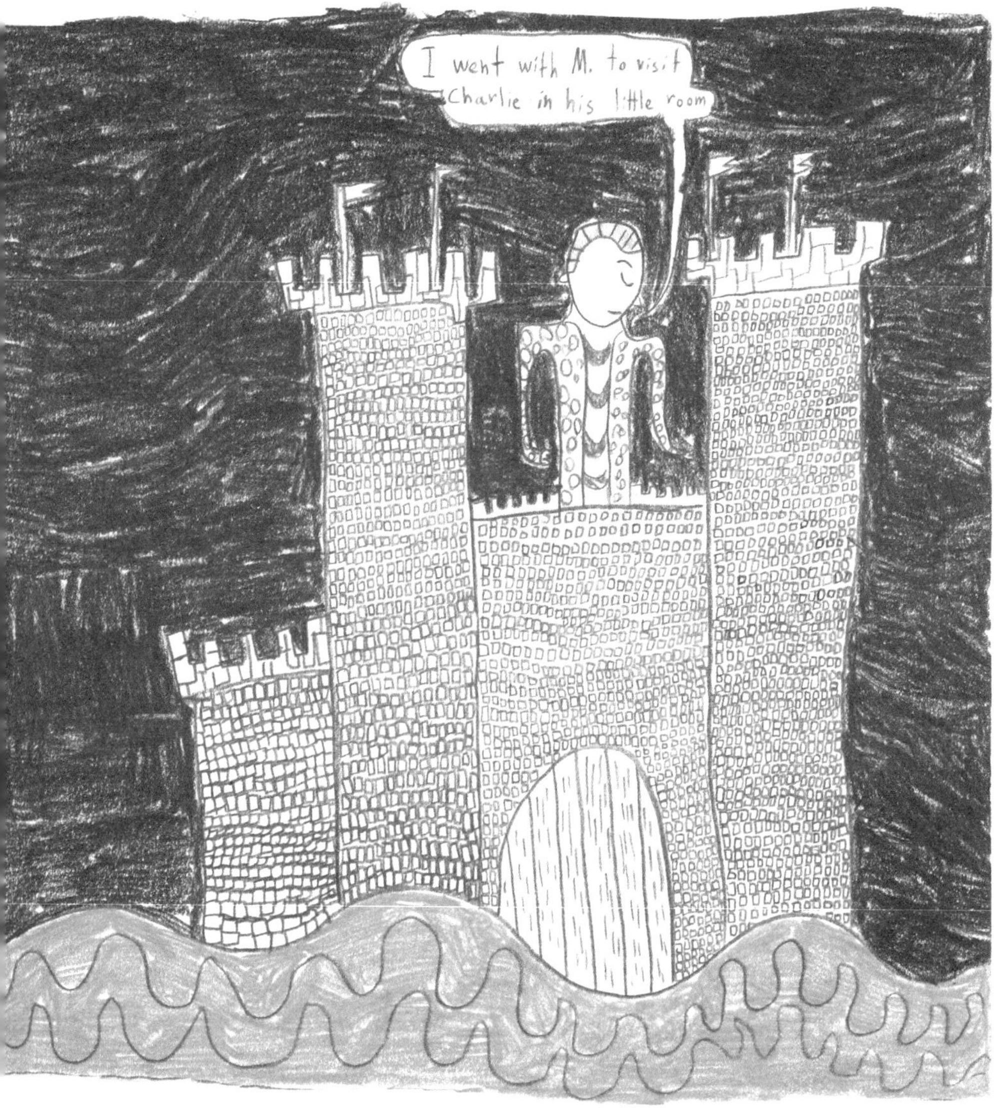
I went with M. to visit
Charlie in his little room

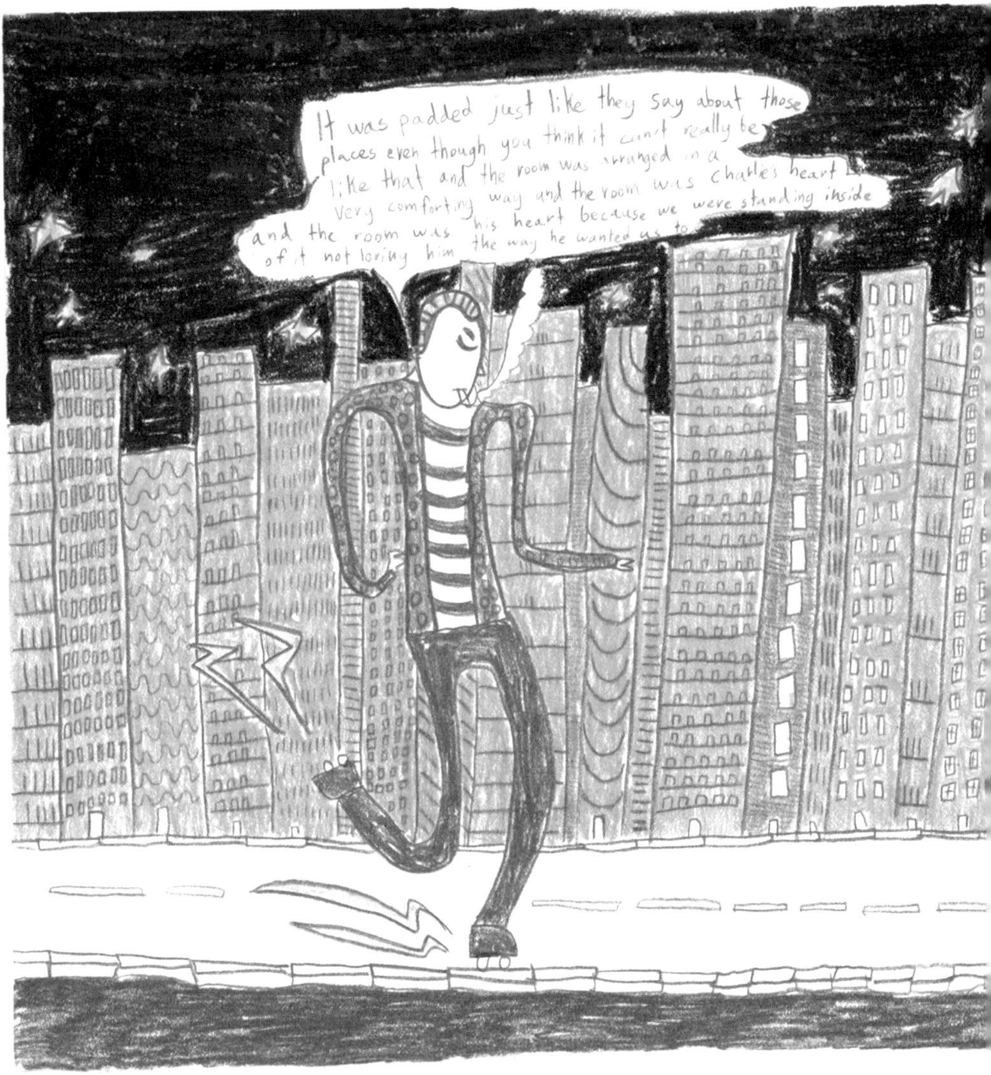
It was padded just like they say about those places even though you think it can't really be like that and the room was arranged in a very comforting way and the room was charlie's heart and the room was his heart because we were standing inside of it not loving him the way he wanted us to

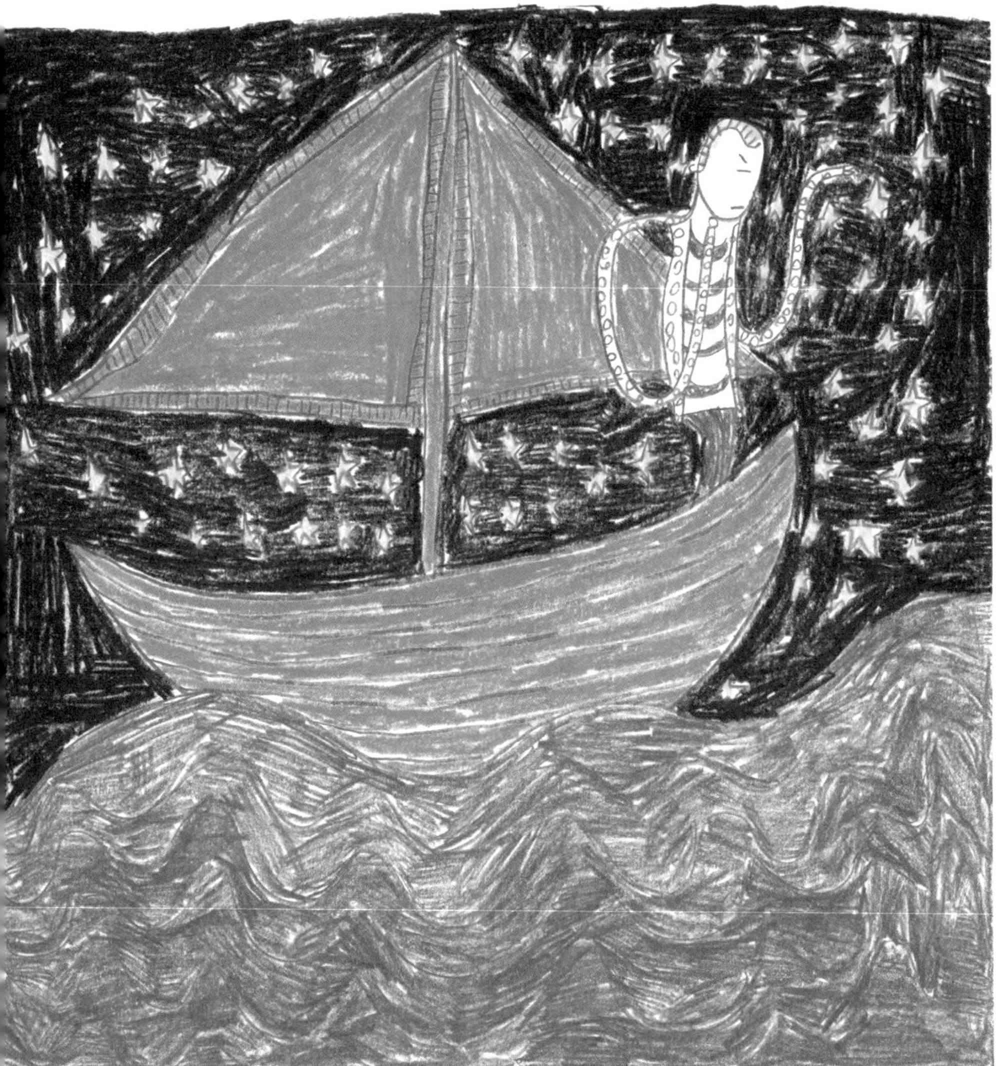

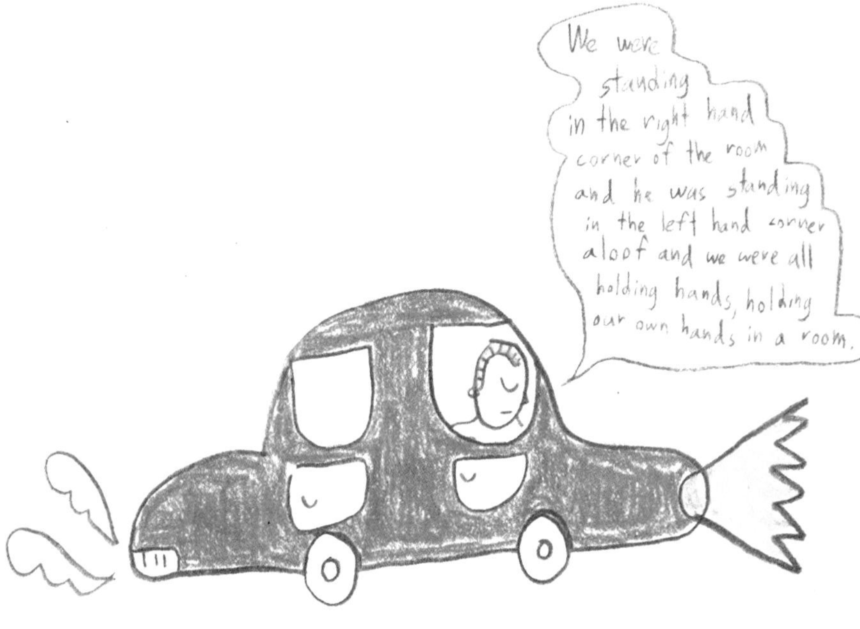
We were standing in the right hand corner of the room and he was standing in the left hand corner aloof and we were all holding hands, holding our own hands in a room.

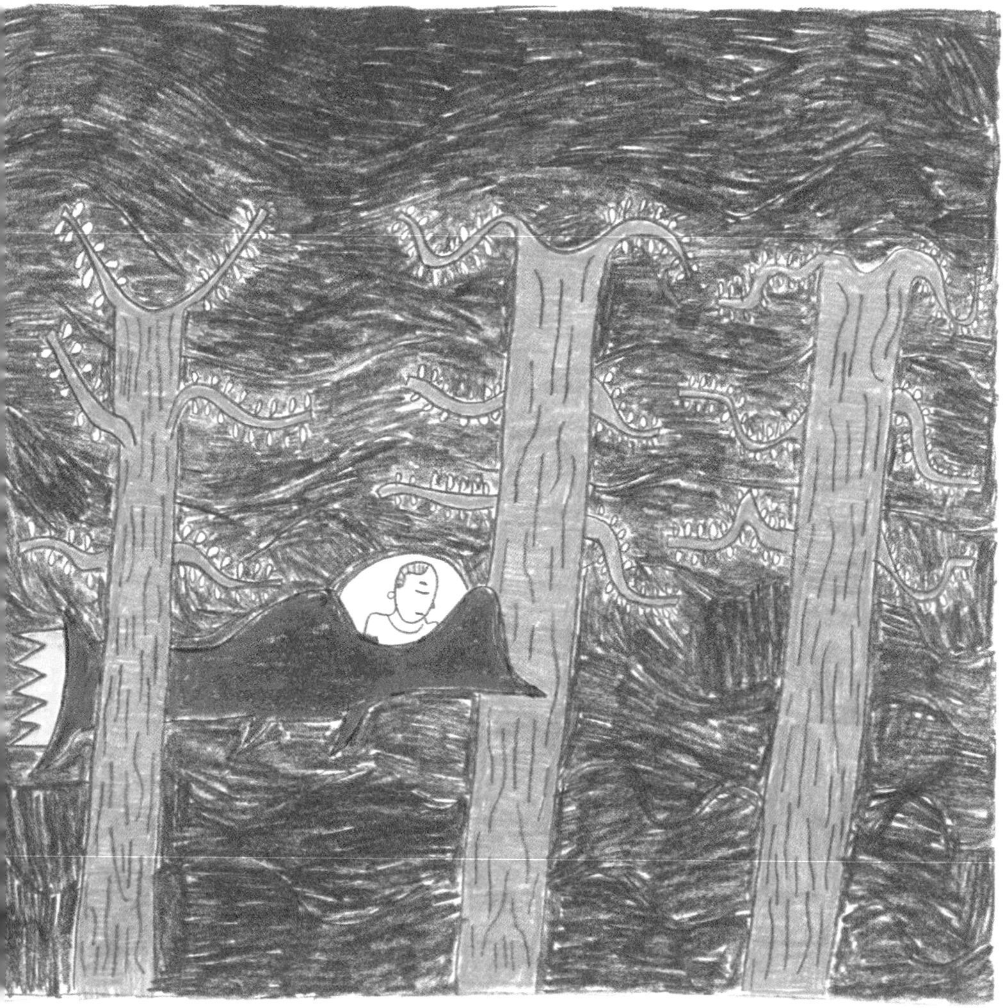

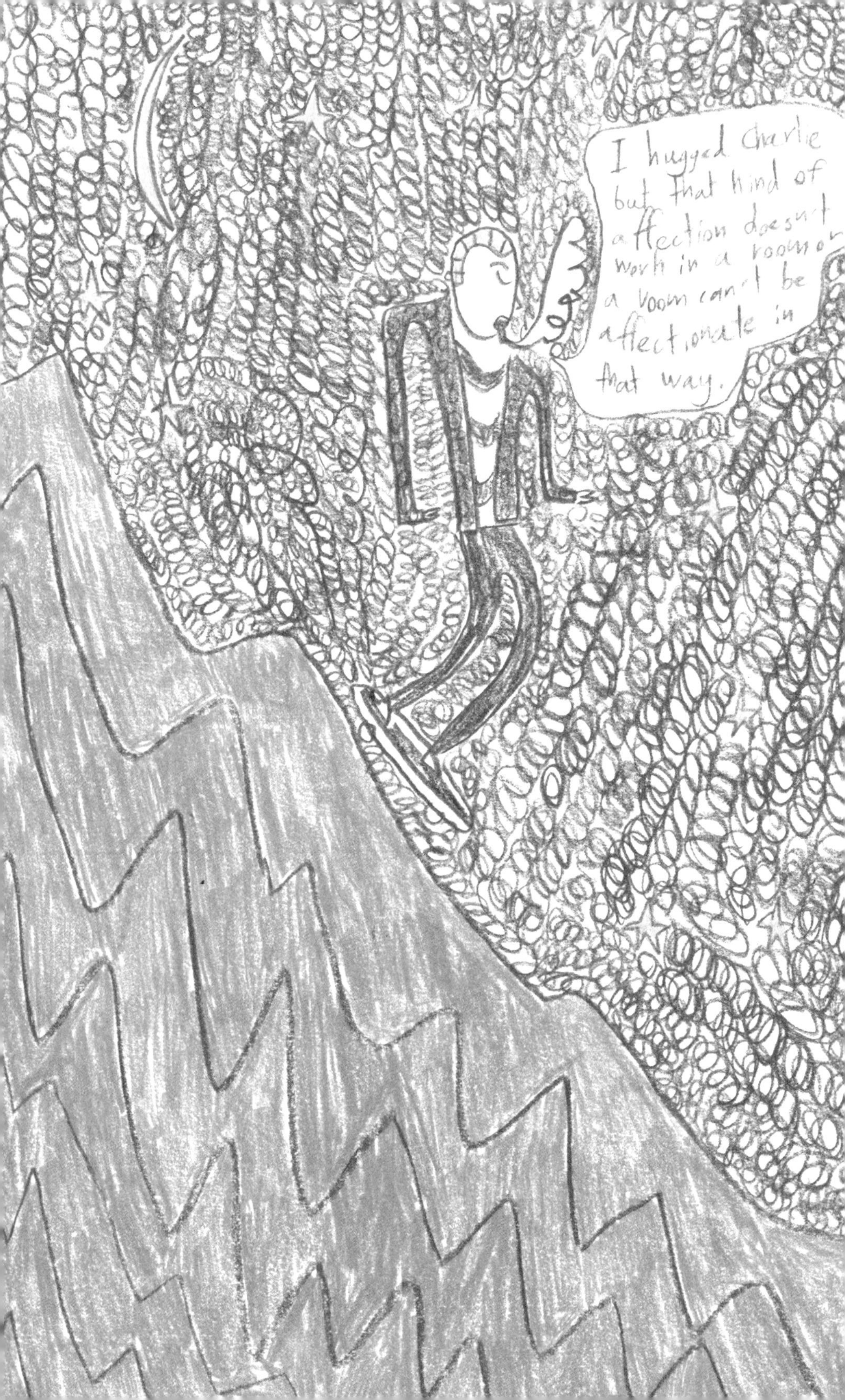
I hugged Charlie but that kind of affection doesn't work in a room or a room can't be affectionate in that way.

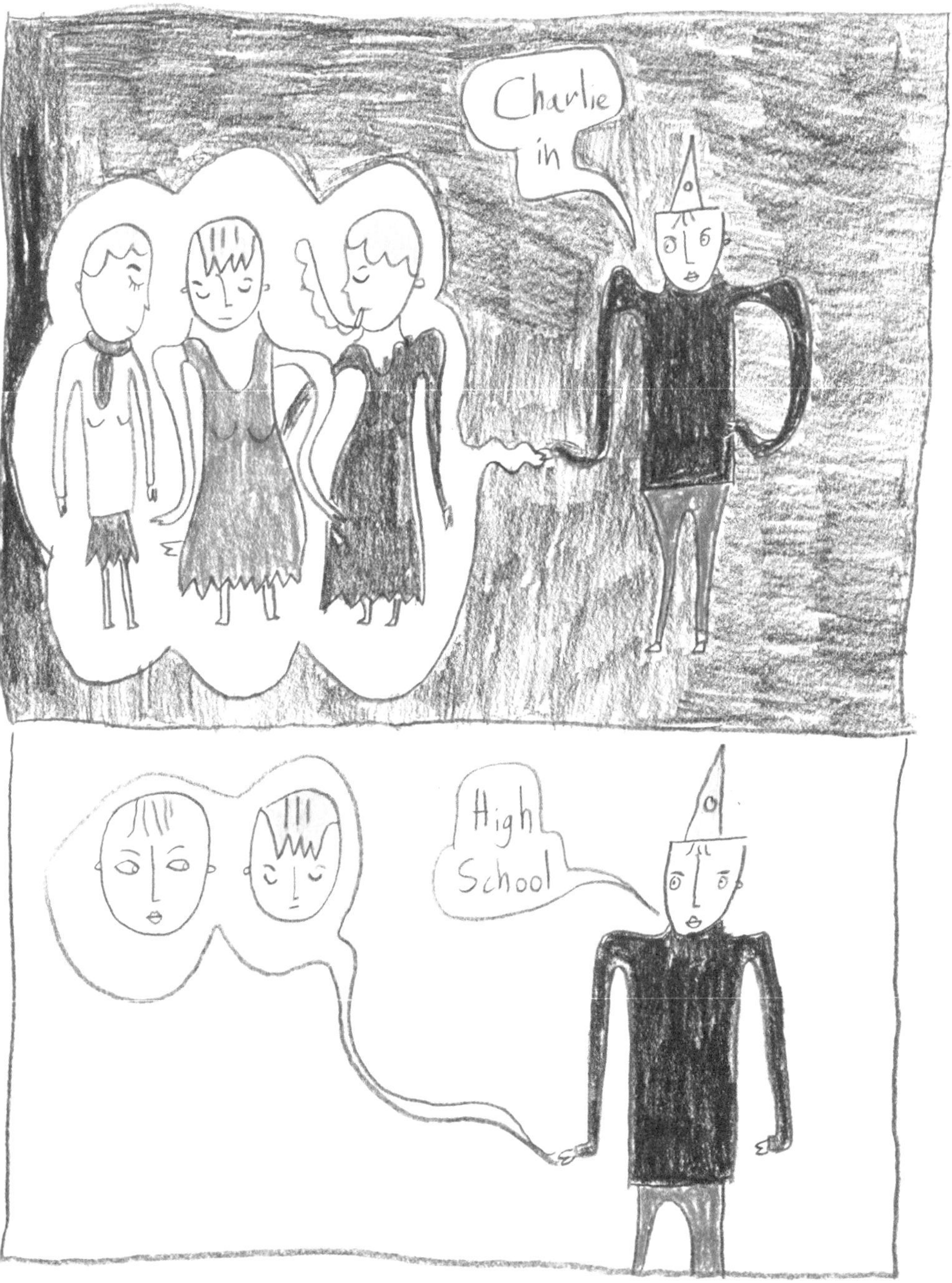
Charlie in
High School

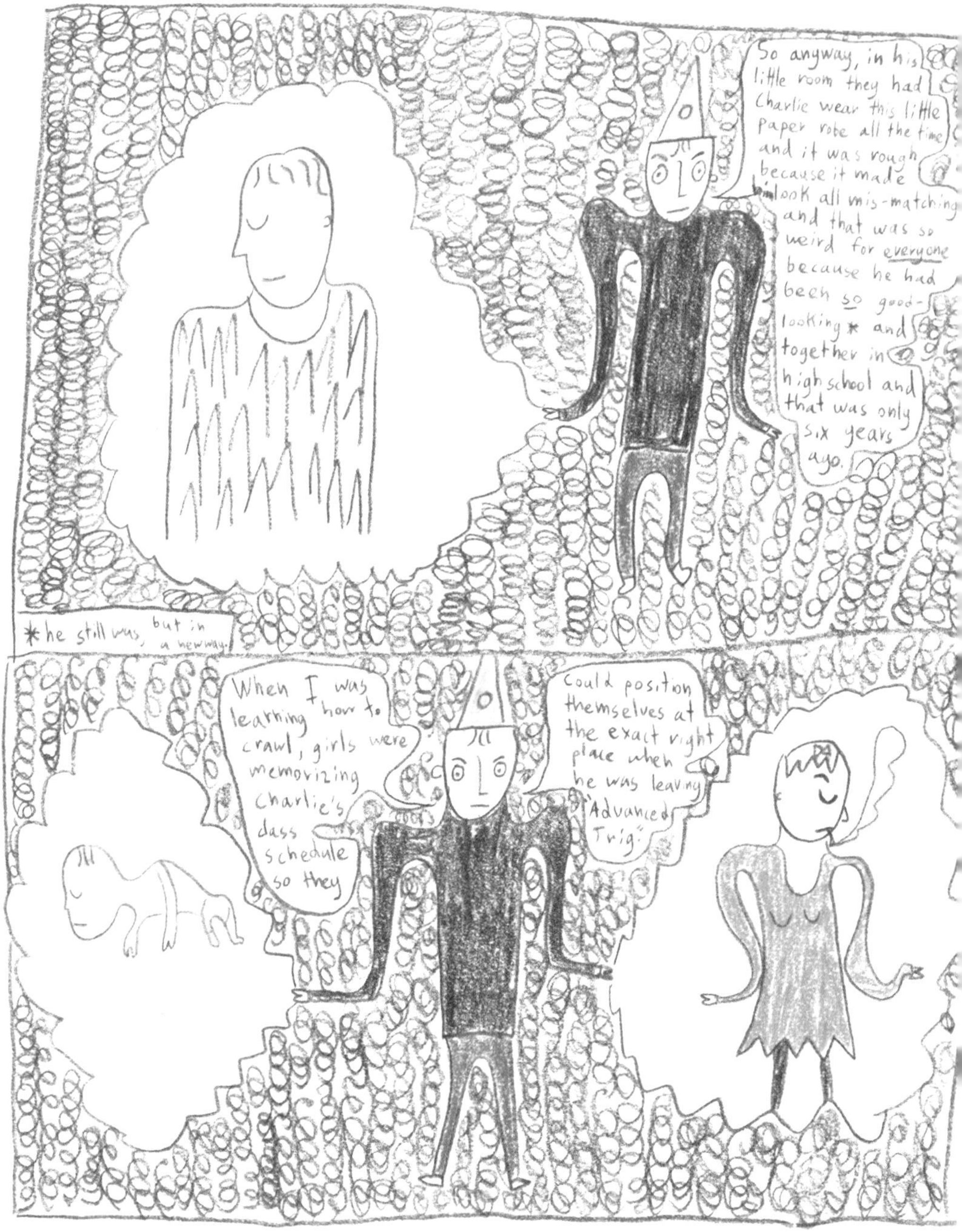
So anyway, in his little room they had Charlie wear this little paper robe all the time and it was rough because it made him look all mis-matching and that was so weird for everyone because he had been so good-looking* and together in high school and that was only six years ago.
* he still was, but in a new way.
When I was learning how to crawl, girls were memorizing Charlie's class schedule so they
Could position themselves at the exact right place when he was leaving "Advanced Trig."

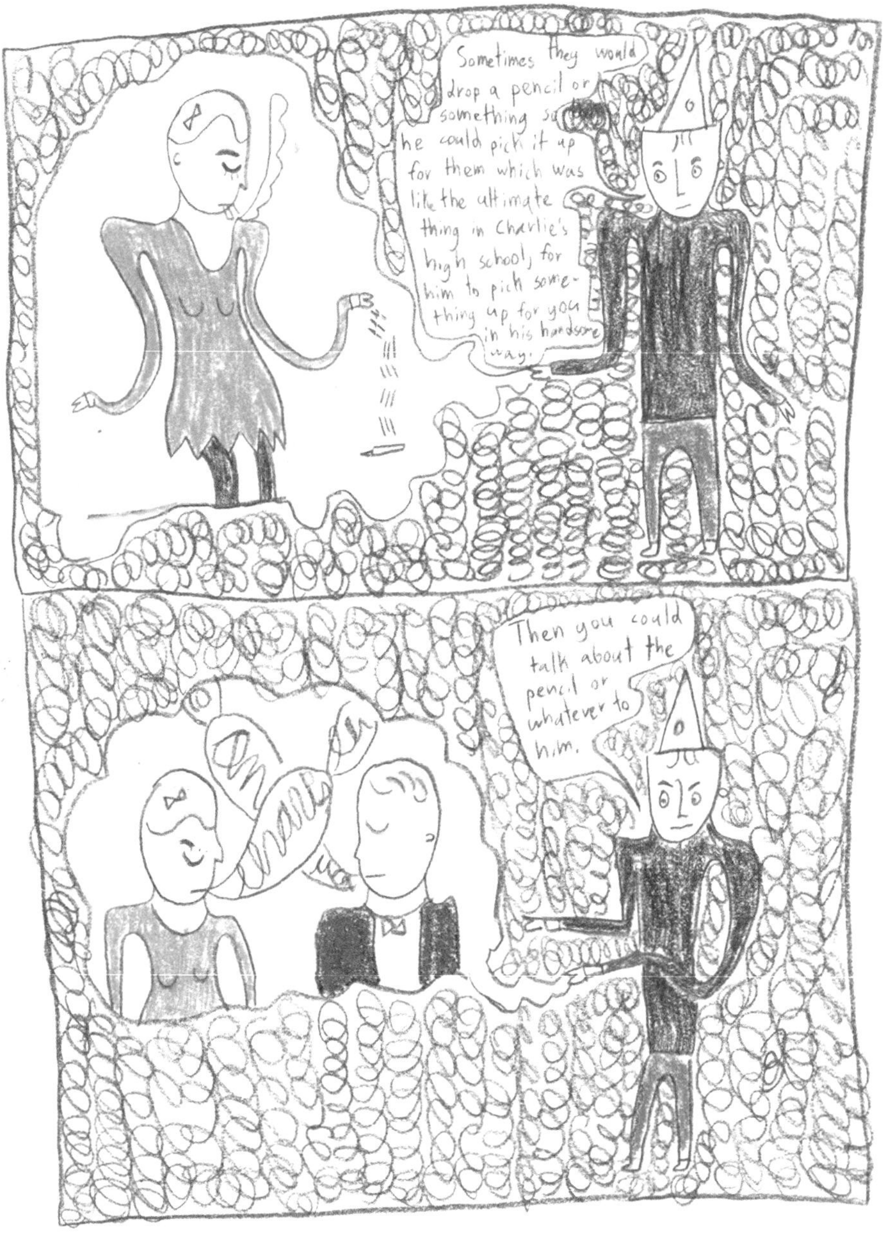
Sometimes they would drop a pencil or something so he could pick it up for them which was like the ultimate thing in Charlie's high school, for him to pick something up for you in his handsome way.
Then you could talk about the pencil or whatever to him.

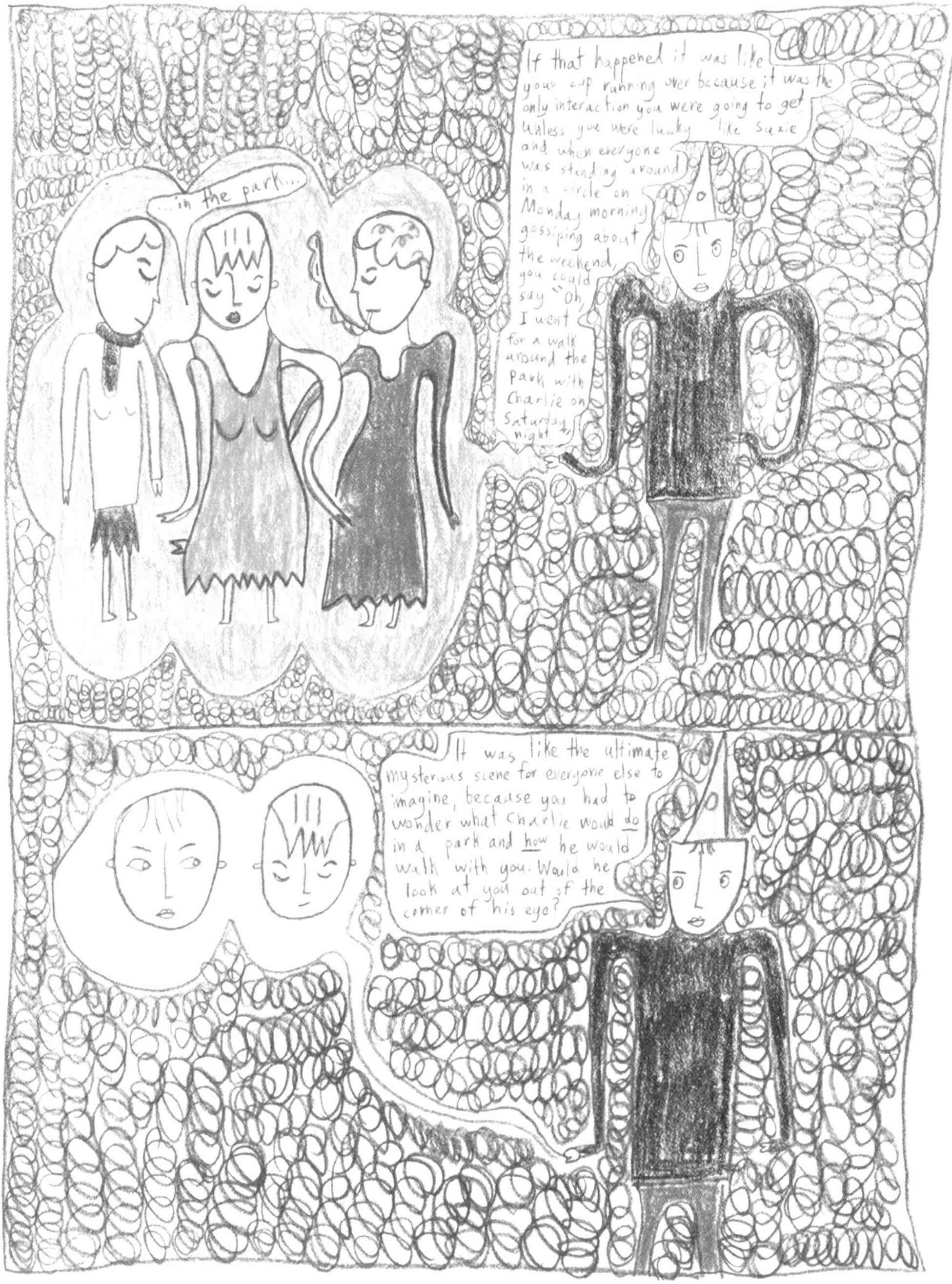
...in the park...
If that happened it was like your cup running over because it was the only interaction you were going to get unless you were lucky like Suzie and when everyone was standing around in a circle on Monday morning gossiping about the weekend, you could say "Oh, I went for a walk around the park with Charlie on Saturday night."
It was like the ultimate mysterious scene for everyone else to imagine, because you had to wonder what Charlie would do in a park and how he would walk with you. Would he look at you out of the corner of his eye?

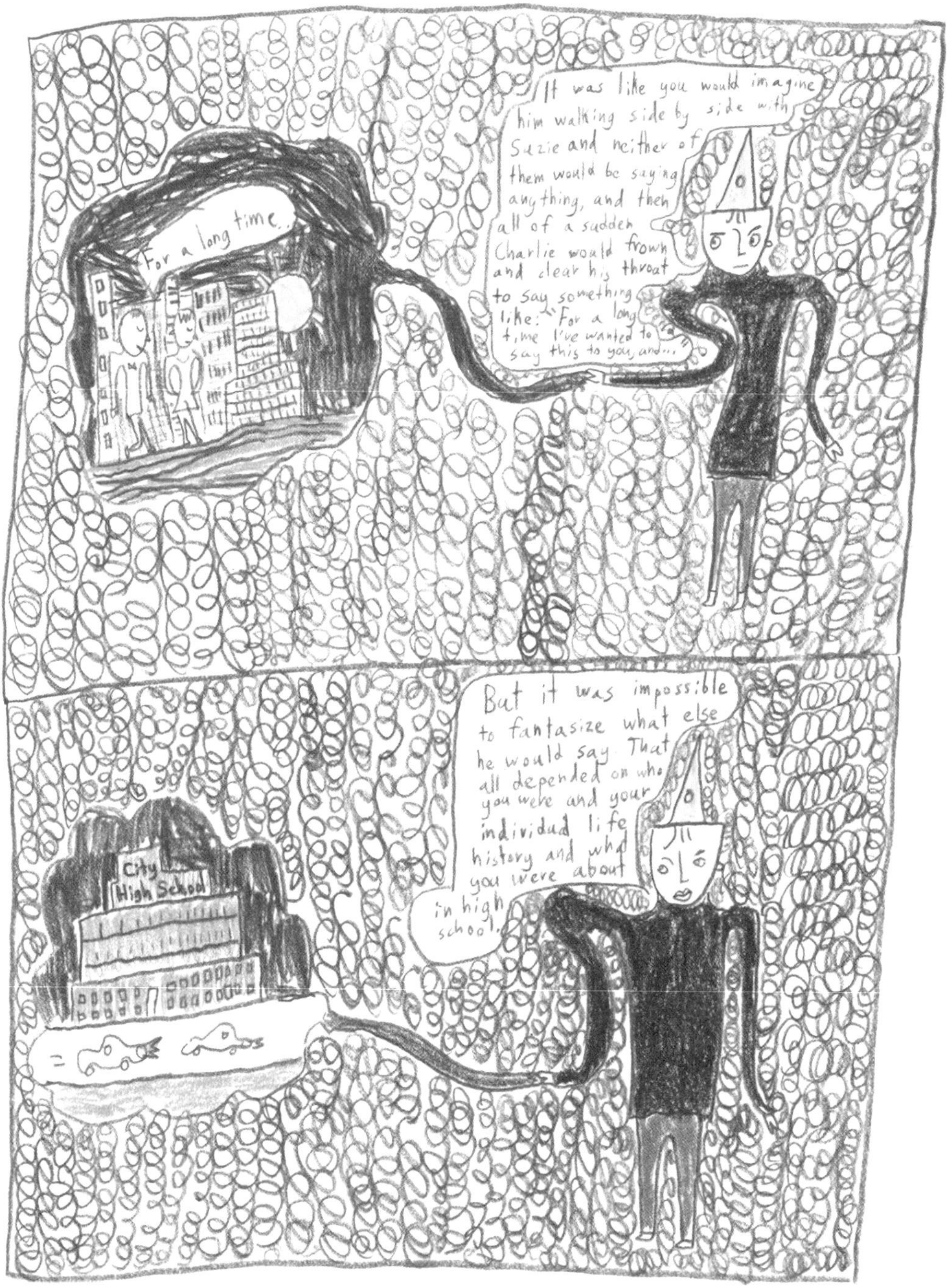

It was like you would imagine him walking side by side with Suzie and neither of them would be saying anything, and then all of a sudden Charlie would frown and clear his throat to say something like: "For a long time I've wanted to say this to you, and...
For a long time...
But it was impossible to fantasize what else he would say. That all depended on who you were and your individual life history and what you were about in high school.
City High School

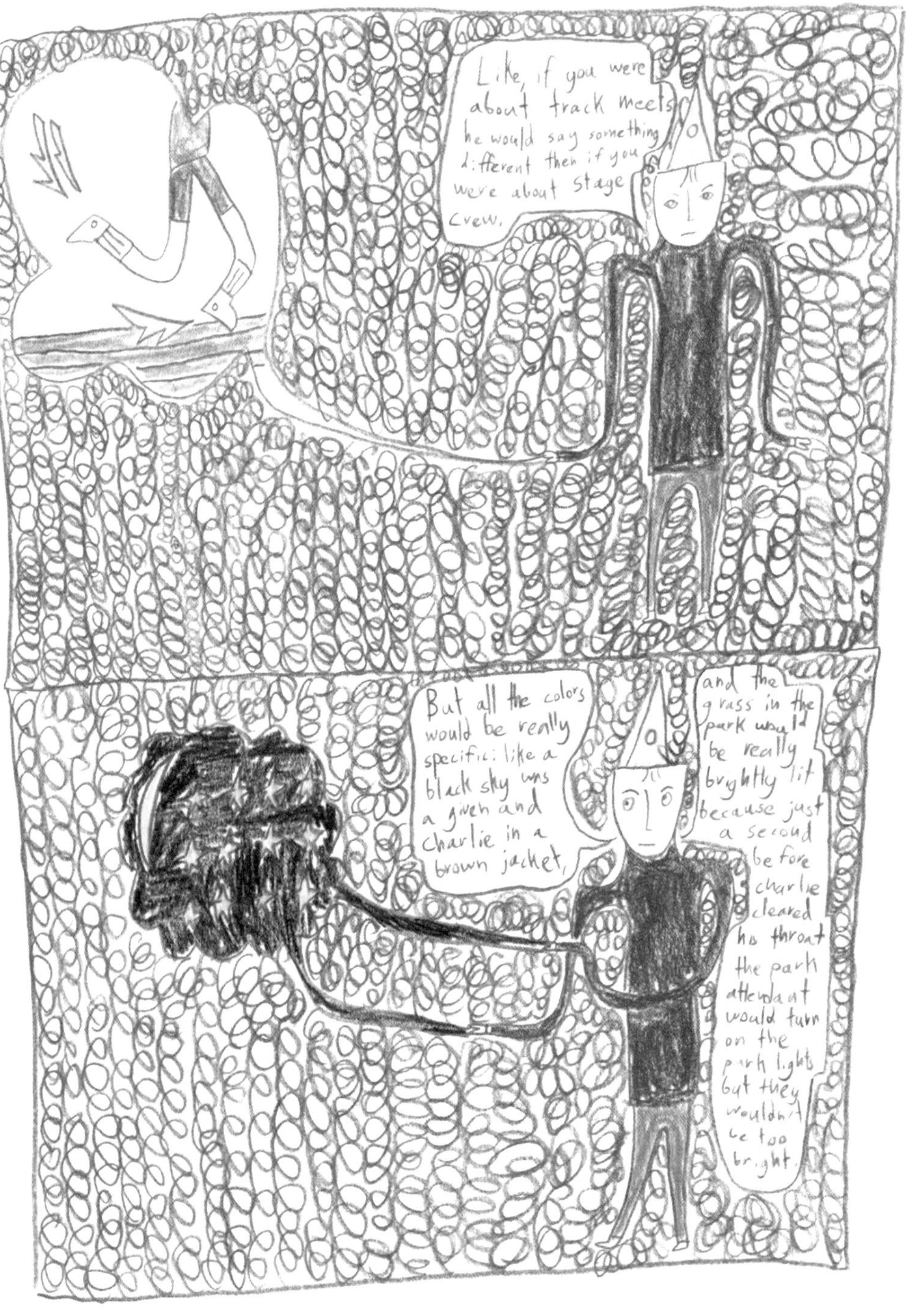
Like, if you were about track meets he would say something different then if you were about stage crew.
But all the colors would be really specific: like a black sky was a given and charlie in a brown jacket,
and the grass in the park would be really brightly lit because just a second before charlie cleared his throat the park attendant would turn on the park lights but they wouldn't be too bright.

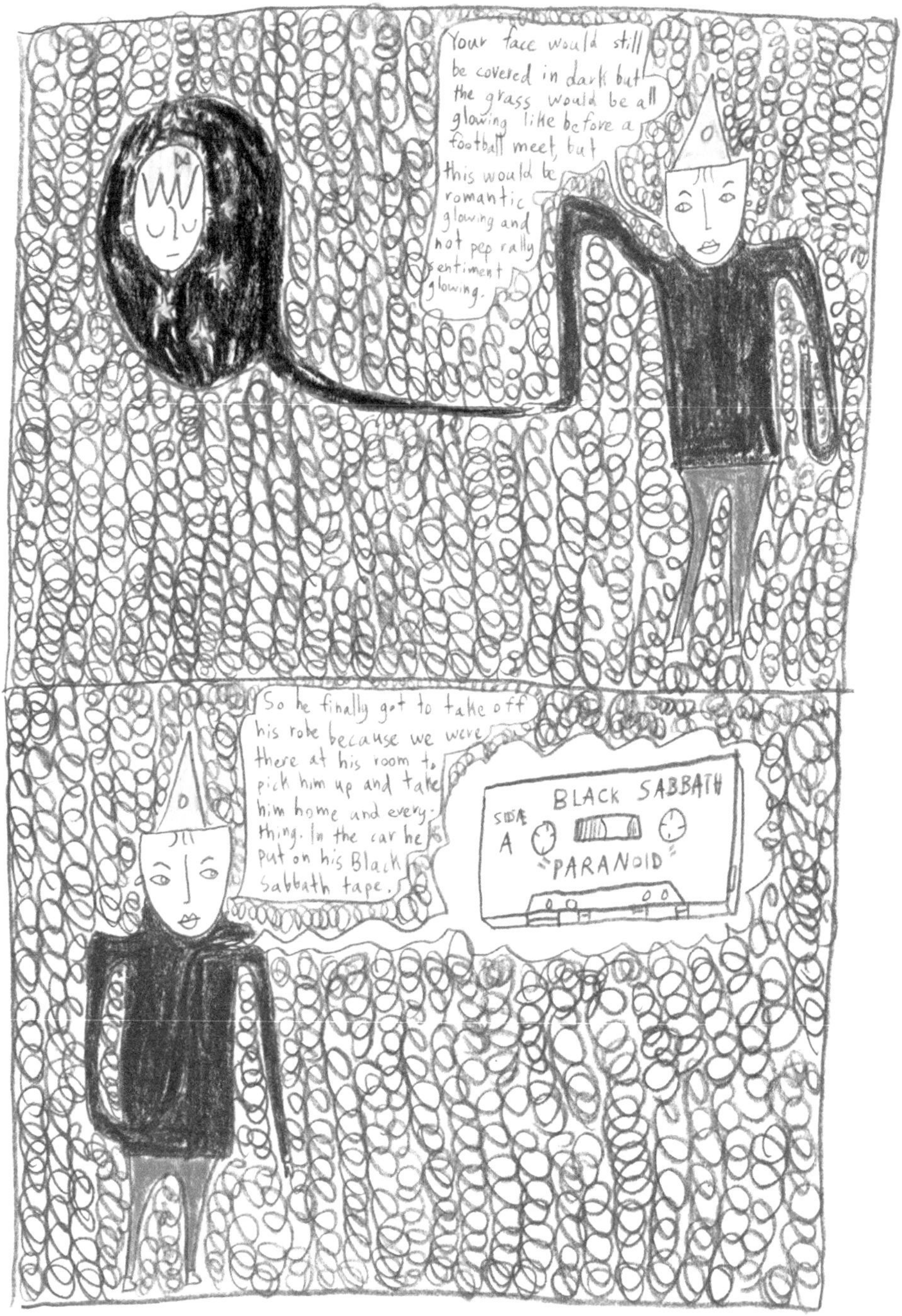
Your face would still be covered in dark but the grass would be all glowing like before a football meet, but this would be romantic glowing and not pep rally sentiment glowing.
So he finally got to take off his robe because we were there at his room to pick him up and take him home and everything. In the car he put on his Black Sabbath tape.
BLACK SABBATH
SIDE A
"PARANOID"

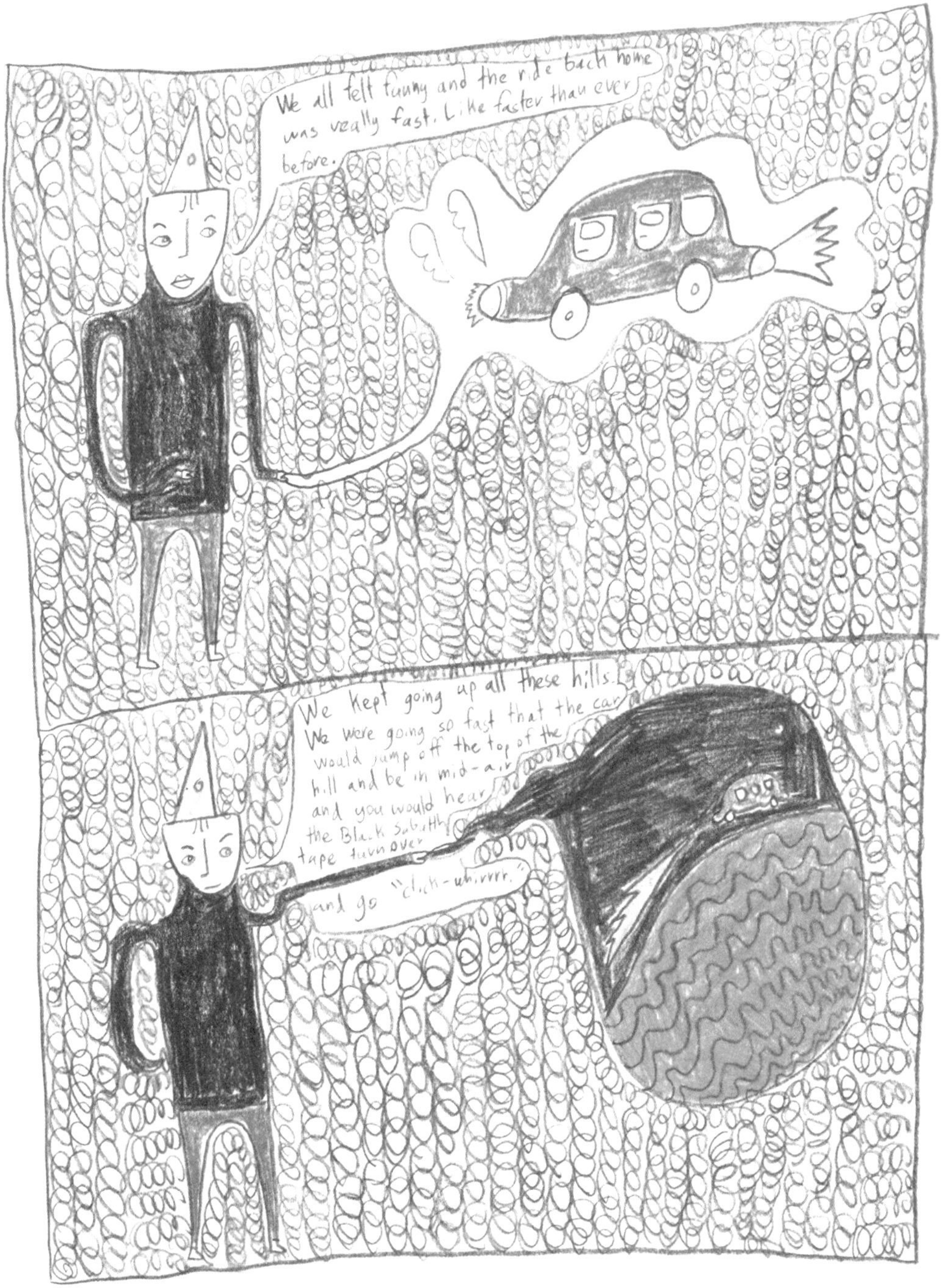
We all felt funny and the ride back home was really fast. Like faster than ever before.
We kept going up all these hills. We were going so fast that the car would jump off the top of the hill and be in mid-air and you would hear the Black Sabbath tape turn over
and go "click-whirrrr."

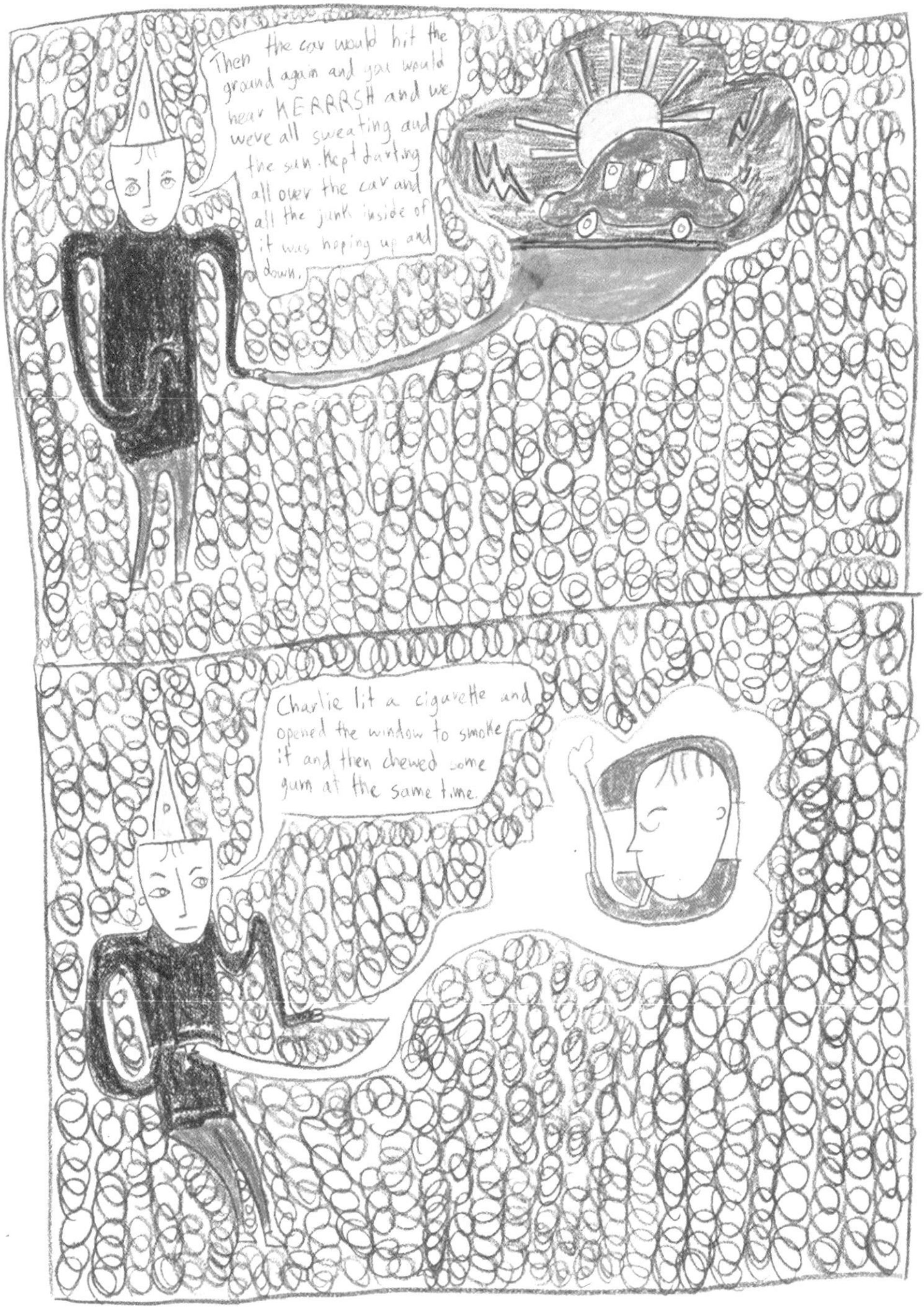
Then the car would hit the ground again and you would hear KERRRSH and we were all sweating and the sun kept darting all over the car and all the junk inside of it was hoping up and down.
Charlie lit a cigarette and opened the window to smoke it and then chewed some gum at the same time.

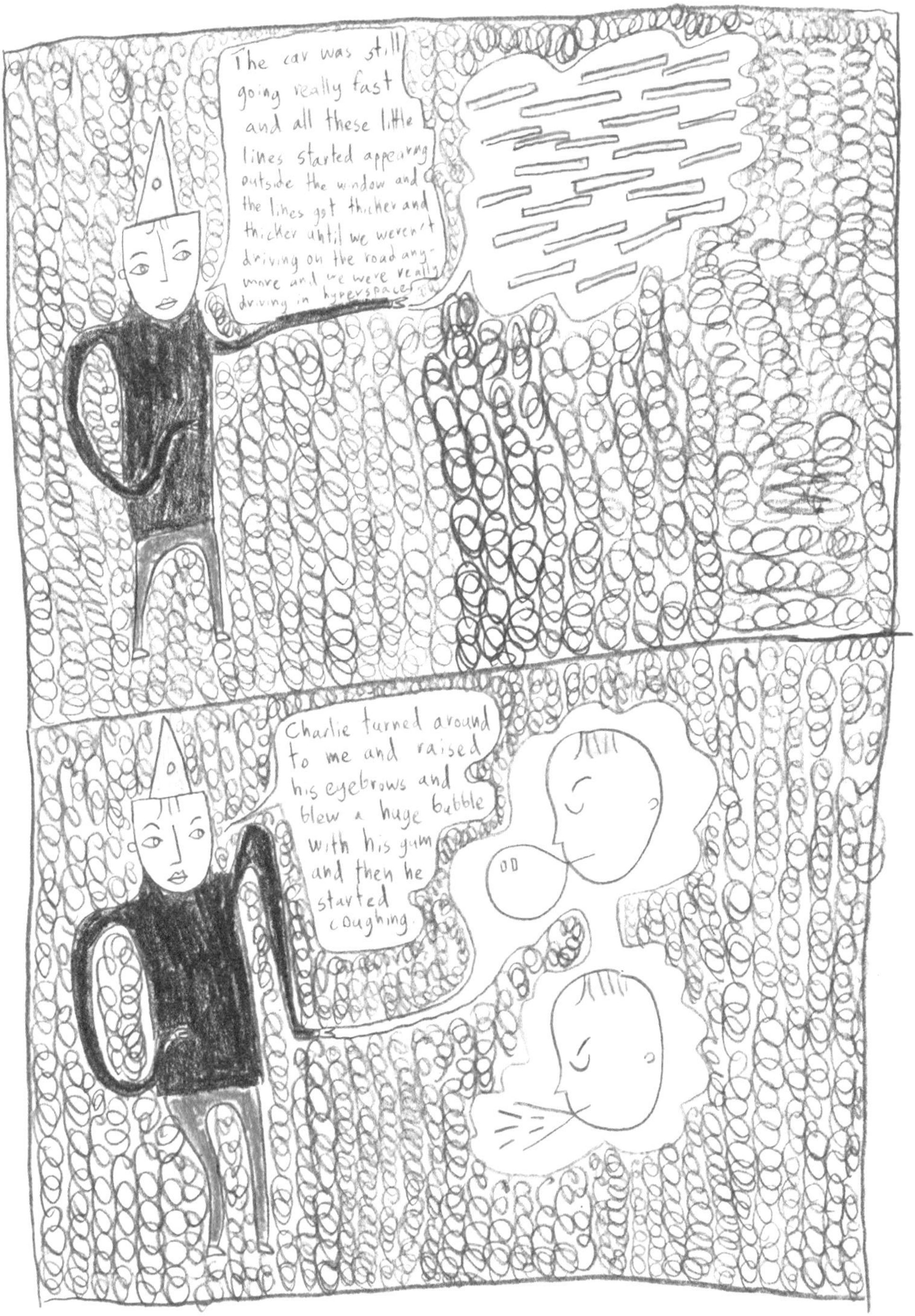
The car was still going really fast and all these little lines started appearing outside the window and the lines got thicker and thicker until we weren't driving on the road any-more and we were really driving in hyperspace.
Charlie turned around to me and raised his eyebrows and blew a huge bubble with his gum and then he started coughing.

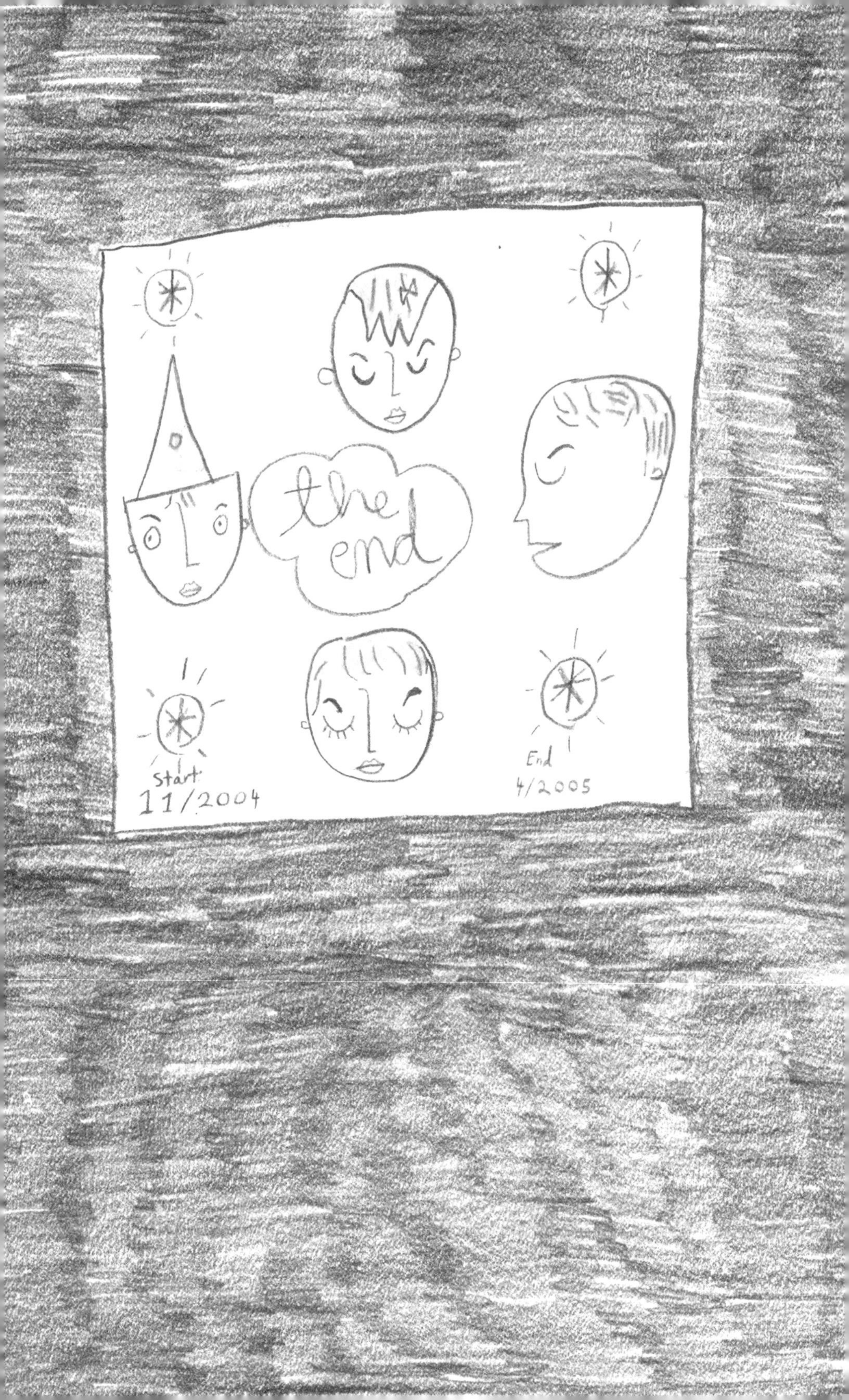

the end
Start:
11/2004
End
4/2005

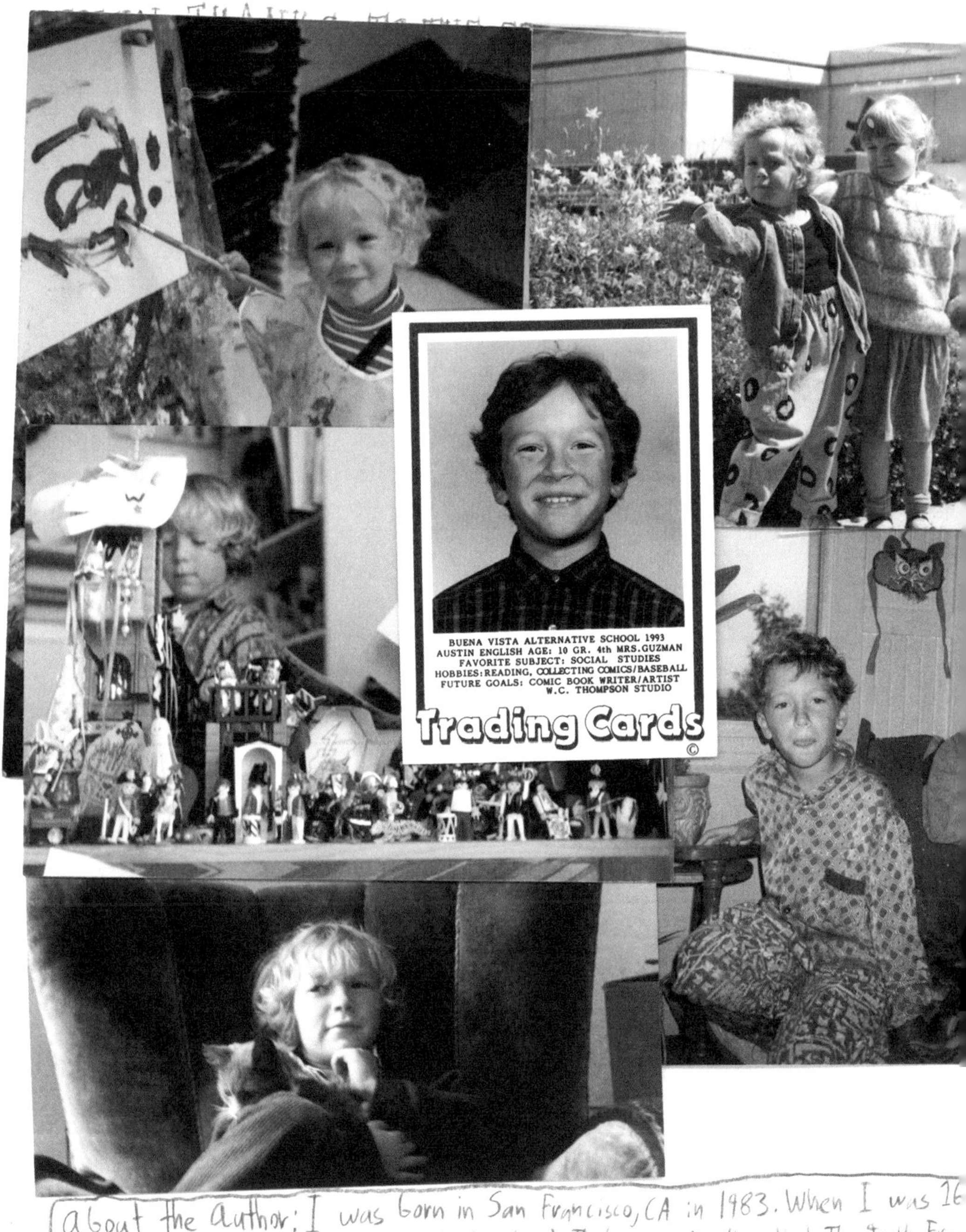
BUENA VISTA ALTERNATIVE SCHOOL 1993
AUSTIN ENGLISH AGE: 10 GR. 4th MRS.GUZMAN
FAVORITE SUBJECT: SOCIAL STUDIES
HOBBIES: READING, COLLECTING COMICS/BASEBALL
FUTURE GOALS: COMIC BOOK WRITER/ARTIST
W.C. THOMPSON STUDIO
Trading Cards
©

About the Author: I was born in San Francisco, CA in 1983. When I was 16 I started self-publishing a comic-book about Thelonious Monk called The Tenth Fra… Now I live in Manhattan and go to classes at The New School for Social Research. This is the first book of many that I'll make in my life. Write to me at: austinenglish337@hotmail.com or mail me a letter at ~~259 W. 11th St, Apt. #2, New York, NY 10014.~~ Thanks for reading this book!

↓ 3604 Grand Ave. Apt #3
Oakland, CA 94610

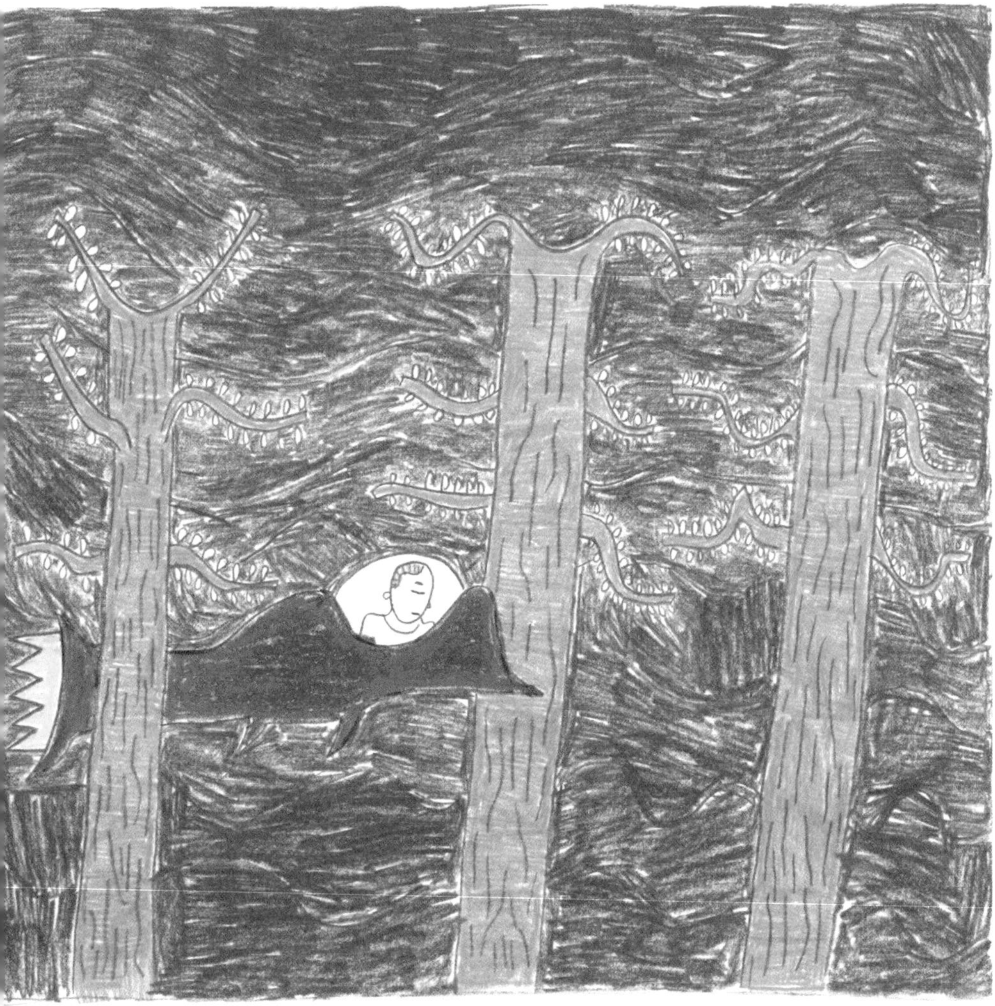

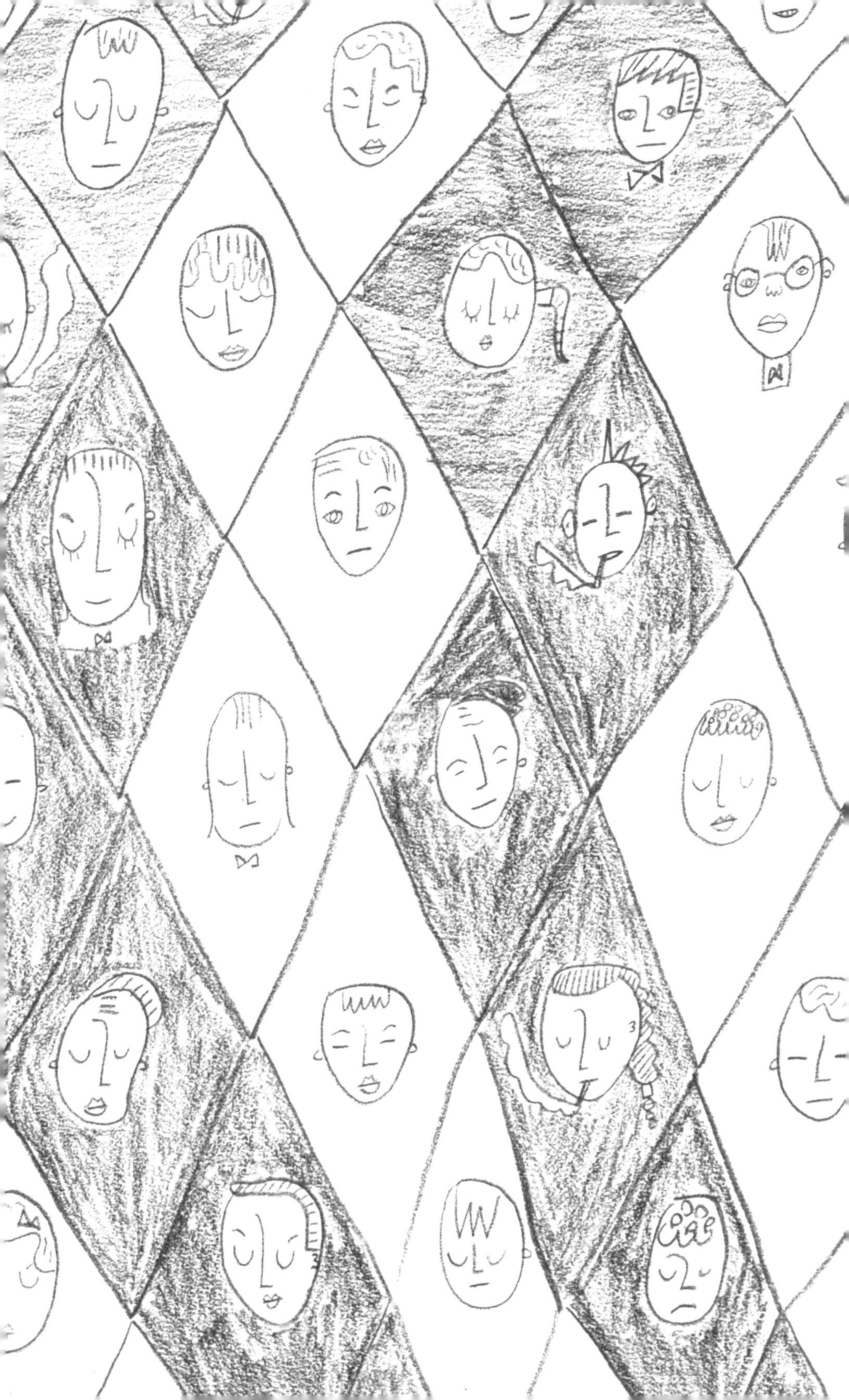